SETTING YOUR HEART

on Fire

SEVEN INVITATIONS

TO LIBERATE

YOUR LIFE

BROADWAY BOOKS NEW YORK

SETTING YOUR HEART

on Fire

RAPHAEL CUSHNIR

PRINTED IN THE UNITED STATES OF AMERICA

BROADWAY BOOKS and its logo, a letter B bisected on the diagonal, are trademarks of Random House, Inc.

Visit our website at www.broadwaybooks.com

First edition published 2003

Book design by Dana Leigh Treglia

Cataloging-in-Publication Data is on file with the Library of Congress.

ISBN 0-7679-1385-X

1   3   5   7   9   10   8   6   4   2

FOR MARIA

Lover, Partner, Goddess, Friend

CONTENTS

INTRODUCTION   1

INVOCATION   5

THE FIRST INVITATION *Feel Everything*   7

THE SECOND INVITATION *Question Everything*   41

THE THIRD INVITATION *Resist Nothing*   71

THE FOURTH INVITATION *Live Like You're Dying*   105

THE FIFTH INVITATION *Live Like You're Dreaming* 137

THE SIXTH INVITATION *Love Like You're Dancing*   173

THE SEVENTH INVITATION *Widen Your World*   215

BENEDICTION   255

GRATITUDE   257

STAYING CONNECTED   259

One day, after we have mastered the winds and the waves and

the tides and gravity, we will harness for God the energies

of love. Then, for the second time in human history,

mankind will have discovered fire.

—PIERRE THEILHARD DE CHARDIN

SETTING YOUR HEART

on Fire

INTRODUCTION

*T*his is a book about love. More books have been written on the subject of love than just about any other. So why one more? The answer lies in a crucial distinction—the love we're about to explore is not romantic, erotic, familial, or platonic. Instead, it exists prior to and apart from any specific type of expression.

This love is a dynamic and primal force. It's the universe's urge for inclusion, for union, for the dissolution of that which separates. Whether subtle or overwhelming, direct or diffuse, its goal is always the same. Love connects.

Love, as we experience it, is sublime. It wells up in the heart, radiates, and brings a glow to our entire being. The sensation is so exquisite we chase after it like the scarcest commodity. We do everything in our power to find it, earn it, win it, keep it. Whether we're aware of it or not, this quest underlies a great many of our other pursuits, even when they seem entirely unrelated.

Early on, however, we make a fateful and costly decision—we won't allow ourselves to feel love unless it appears in the guise of our desire. When our parents disapprove of us or abandon us, we shrink from love like it's the actual culprit. When our beloved doesn't meet us in our ardor, suddenly the world seems barren, devoid of love. So, too, with failure, with loss, with all of life's major disappointments. They tap that secret place inside where we fear, or have already come to believe, that the real blame for our misfortune lies with us. We judge ourselves unlucky, unworthy, unlovable.

Our overwhelming need for love, ironically, can often blind us to its constant presence. In fact love is here, always, regardless of our circumstance and dependent upon absolutely nothing. Allow me to share an open secret—love is waiting for you. Not in the form you may expect, or believe you need, but instead without form at all. It's an aspect of the divine, permeating all of creation, and it never says "no."

We ask the world of love. In truth, we demand it. But rarely do we stop to consider what love requires of us.

Isn't it about time?

Before going any further, I'd like to explain how this book came to be. In 1995, after a period of profound grief, I experienced a personal and spiritual transformation. What I learned from that transformation was described five years later in my first book, *Unconditional Bliss: Finding Happiness in the Face of Hardship*. The book explains a simple process for becoming more present in any moment, especially the most difficult ones, and for breaking through persistent blocks. This process is call Living the Questions, and since introducing it I've been traveling the United States nonstop. As I live the questions with people in workshops, retreats, schools, spiritual centers, and private homes, I'm always humbled by the courage they display in healing their deepest wounds.

In the wake of their self-healing, many of these people are filled with a new appreciation for the very lives they recently resisted. In place of bitterness and frustration, they often feel great love toward everyone and everything, even those who have hurt them the most. When this love fades in the crush of daily life, as is usually the case, not surprisingly they want it back. They want to know how to make this love last, and how to share it with others for the highest good of all.

At first, faced with their requests, I felt unqualified to answer. How could I, or anyone for that matter, presume to speak for love? But then a voice called from within—*Listen to your heart*. While this could have been a metaphor, I decided to take it literally. It helped that I was aware of recent scientific research demonstrating that the heart has its own intelligence, its own way of communicating. Encouraged by that awareness I listened, waited, and prayed for the ability to tune in.

What came to me, therefore, was really not my own. Yet neither was it "channeled" or arrived at in any esoteric way. I simply sat, and wrote, and used whatever skills I could muster to translate my heart's wisdom into language. Along the way I came to understand that there is only one heart—love's heart—and that all of us are joined within it. Our task is less to learn than to remember. So I offer this book in that spirit, as much reader as author, hoping that it stirs you as it does me, and stands as a reminder of the unity we are.

WHAT LOVE WANTS

As the new century dawns, the world grows ever smaller and more interconnected. People of all races, classes, and continents are affected. Such globalization brings many benefits, but also immense friction. There are fewer resources to consume and far greater competition for them. Ideologies clash. Epidemics rage. Terrorism looms. Both our friends and foes live right among us, and it's often difficult to tell them apart. Isolation, once a reasonable choice for both nations and individuals, has now become a quaint fantasy. Today we find as much fear as hope, as much sorrow as joy, and as much danger as opportunity.

It would be a grave mistake to view this reality as solely political. No new policy or military campaign can ever provide lasting security. As long as we believe that we're fundamentally separate from one another, matters can only get worse. The battle for the twenty-first century, therefore, is personal. It will be won or lost within each of us, a single heart at a time.

Scores of people already understand this. They've begun to take stock of themselves in the deepest ways. This may or may not involve a religion, an institution, or an affiliation of any kind. But it always seeks to unravel the strictures of one's past, illuminate shadows, and unleash the power of a fully authentic life.

This is what love wants. But it's only the beginning.

To live in accord with love is to set your heart on fire. In the crucible of such an inferno all convention burns away. What's left is an entirely new kind of existence, one full of passion, presence, and infinite possibility.

The Invitations that follow are sparks to ignite your blaze. The Illuminations that accompany them are winds to fan your flames. As you open yourself to this searing light, love will inevitably engulf you. You won't just understand it, or feel it, but will come to *embody* love in everything you say and do.

This loving embodiment is as practical as it is poetic. While it will certainly bring a new luster to moments of intimacy, it will also change the way you meet stress and adversity. Love will lead the way when you may have come to expect it least—in times of anxiety, depression, loneliness, illness, pain, and conflict.

THE PATH OF A LIFETIME

The triumph of love, though all encompassing, does not transpire at once. Each Invitation requires significant patience and practice. After reading them all to get the big picture, you may want to go back to the beginning and delve into them one by one. Especially at first, many of the shifts in perspective they entail can seem quite difficult. They will require a candid reassessment of your deepest beliefs and most ingrained behaviors. If any of these beliefs and behaviors are barring you from your greatest access to love, you'll be instructed how to transform them step by step.

These steps can often create "growing pains," or brief periods of frustration and disorientation. It might take a full month or more before each Invitation feels natural and fully your own. It might help to discuss the Invitations with friends or in a structured group. Even then, however, many of the most significant results will arrive subtly and gradually. In fact, embraced together, the Seven Invitations are the spiritual path of an entire lifetime.

Keeping this long view in mind will greatly enhance your journey. Otherwise you may go too fast, try too hard, or demand more of yourself than necessary. Any of these approaches will create tension and self-opposition, which you'll soon see only stand in love's way.

The Invitations are each designed to strike a delicate balance, meeting you exactly where you are without losing sight of all you're meant to become. Accepting them in your own time will make you stronger, wiser, and kinder. It will liberate your life by calling forth your very best.

Are you ready?

INVOCATION

Love, speak to me

Render me willing

Receptive

Humble enough to hear your words

Strong enough to live your light

To meet your gaze in all things

To bless them, join them,

In your sacred heart of hearts

THE FIRST INVITATION

Feel Everything

Sometimes we kill our heart

in order not to feel.

—TENNESSEE WILLIAMS

In the First Invitation, love calls you to experience

your emotions fully. To do so requires learning

when and why you deny them, and developing the

capacity for reconnection.

*T*o love is to open. To love fully is to open wide. When we're wide open, love rushes toward us and emanates from us. We recognize it as the essence of our existence. Naturally, without effort, the illusion of separation vanishes. We experience ourselves as part of one great whole, indistinguishable from all we survey.

Too often, however, we shrink from the experience of oneness and then get used to it. We come to mistake the lie of limitation for the boundless truth of love. We let ourselves love family, friends, and country, but stop there. We offer our love to God, but withhold it from much of divine creation. Yet none of this is irreversible. Nothing, outside of our own unwillingness, can keep us from reconnecting.

Think of the first time you fell in love. Remember how everything was somehow different, how the entire universe seemed to harmonize with joyful intent? Your senses were heightened, your blood quickened. Daily annoyances became sources of awe. Difficult people seemed suddenly wonderful. All your problems, a moment ago insurmountable, now felt like the smallest hurdle.

Sadly, it didn't last. It rarely does. But for however long you're rapt, falling in love causes you to remember the vastness of love's reach. Afterward, if you're like most people, you quickly begin seeking the next one who will supposedly, miraculously, return you to that rapture for good.

But you *can* feel such rapture all the time. Love is yours without a partner, without any object whatsoever, once you're willing to feel everything. To accept the First Invitation means approaching every single moment as you would a lover. You don't just feel the moment but lean into it, let it roar right through you, and meet it with equal intensity.

When a moment brings pleasure, such openness is easy. But when it brings frustration or pain, your likely reaction is the exact opposite. You close off, shut down. A shutdown is your instinctive response to any emotion that you don't like or don't want. It's your way of saying either "Get these feelings away from me," or "Get me away from them."

Whenever you shut down, you become unavailable to love. Though this initial response is unavoidable, you can always choose to move beyond it. To do so requires welcoming all your emotions, even the most difficult. In doing so you inevitably reopen, gaining immediate access to love even while challenging times continue. As you embrace the fullness of life, with all its trials and traumas, love embraces you in return.

All of this happens only in the present, one moment at a time. To determine whether you are open or closed, you must bring your awareness into the present. The simplest way to do this is by turning your attention to your body, and by learning to detect the stress patterns that indicate a shutdown. These stress patterns exist in the body because that's where emotions exist as well. As part of their nature, emotions strive to flow through the body as quickly as possible. And they always succeed, unless you block them by shutting down. While in a shutdown you may find yourself scowling, tensing your shoulders, holding your breath, or all of the above. Each of us is unique in our signs and symptoms, but the more you look for them the more easily they become apparent.

Look. Keep looking. Look so often that the very first indication of a shutdown sounds a bell through your whole being.

Regardless of how it manifests, a shutdown means only one thing—there's an emotion you're not feeling. Why aren't you feeling it? Because you're afraid. You're afraid that feeling it will be worse than not feeling it. But in reality that's seldom the case. While you can certainly choose to avoid situations that may elicit a particular feeling, you can't protect yourself from a feeling once it arises. Any attempt at such protection, even when well intentioned, will only serve to keep you shut down.

The need to feel is a basic human trait, as vital as the requirement for food. Most of us would never consider self-starvation, yet we starve ourselves emotionally on a daily basis.

We tell endless stories about why we can't or shouldn't feel. *I'm too weak*, for instance, or *I'm too busy*, or *Everyone will think I'm a wreck*. Some stories have to do with how we see ourselves, and some with how other people see us. But all stories point toward one fundamental truth—surrendering to unwanted feelings means giving up our sense of self-control. This applies whether we avoid most feelings, or have learned to accept all but a few.

We can't control our feelings because they're part of our very life force. They have a powerful will of their own, like the currents in a rushing river. We never know how long we'll feel insulted, or hopeless, or vengeful, or lonely. This unpredictability is as frustrating as it is inconvenient. So instead of letting feelings just sweep through us we gird ourselves against them, attempting to keep the whole uncontrollable mess far away, out there.

The problem is that feelings are never out there, they're always *in here*. And once we're locked down there's absolutely nowhere for them to go. Unwanted feelings become stagnant, foul, and ultimately poisonous. All those supposed victories of self-control against wayward emotion turn into defeats with names like depression, cancer, obesity, heart disease, and stroke.

Yet, of course, you know all this. On some level you always have. Which is why it's so easy to ignore. Which is why it's the First Invitation. The other six Invitations are built upon this commitment to emotional presence. Without it they are mere words, dry and austere ideals.

Once you recognize how vital it is to feel everything, three key distinctions arise. First, feeling everything is not the same as *expressing* everything. You may often shy away from feeling because you confuse the two, imagining that allowing your emotions to flow leads to melodrama and narcissism. While sometimes nothing could be more appropriate than sobbing, raging, leaping with joy, or singing at the top of your lungs, at other times such extroversion doesn't fit. And love, in its wisdom, leaves the decision to you. Sometimes venting your feelings might seem selfish, reactive, or counterproductive. That's why you're always free to assess the situation and then decide whether to express yourself now, later, or not at all.

Second, feeling everything is not the same as *exaggerating* everything. Such exaggeration can take many forms. You may hold on to feelings after they're ready to depart, instead of allowing them to take their natural course. You may analyze feelings to the point of obsession, rather than just letting them be. You may become overemotional in a way that's not quite genuine, forgetting that everyone experiences feelings uniquely. None of these exaggerations is in keeping with the First Invitation. In fact, manipulating the free flow of feeling is a subtle way of rejecting it.

Finally, feeling everything is not the same as *enduring* everything. There's no need for it to render you stuck, or passive, or victimized by circumstances you can change. Emotional presence actually ensures the opposite. It invigorates you, tapping into the storehouse of energy that feelings possess. By remaining open you become more creative, more attuned to what's in your own best interest. Often, once your feelings come into focus, the right path of action suddenly does, too.

Emotional presence also keeps you from "acting out." This term, employed so often in regard to children, has even more relevance for adults. It means using your actions to demonstrate what you're unable to feel or express directly. This may apply to the smallest act, like making a nasty remark instead of communicating the hurt that gave rise to it. But it also may apply to a major event, like having an affair to convey marital rage. In truth, many people spend their entire lives acting out. The urgency of their external goals holds a clue to what roils within. A desperate need for wealth, for example, may arise from deep-seated insecurity. The drive for fame or status, likewise, often stems from feelings of worthlessness.

Considering these last two examples, you may wonder what's so bad about acting out. If shutdowns around insecurity and worthlessness can lead to wealth and fame, wouldn't that be turning a negative into a positive? It would if the motivating feelings went away, but they rarely do. The same achievements that might provide real satisfaction for other people, in these cases ring mostly hollow.

When it comes to feelings, the only way out is through. It's that simple. The beauty of opening to all feelings, even the ones we judge as negative, is that in time they let go of *us*. At the start feeling everything can seem like annihilation, like being engulfed by wave after emotional wave. But actually the reverse is true. In giving up our illusion of self-control, we gain a lasting sense of authenticity. This authenticity gives rise to greater power, freedom, and an astonishing revelation:

The more we feel, the more we love. And the more we love, the more love becomes us.

ILLUMINATING THE

FIRST INVITATION

The master gives himself up to

whatever the moment brings.

—LAO TSE

BREAKING OPEN

Recognizing the shutdown of feelings
is how emotional presence begins.

*I*n order to open to your feelings, you need to pay attention to them. Paying attention to what you're feeling is a simple act. It's simple, but not easy. To pay attention consistently requires breaking habits that may have developed over decades. Even those who have become highly skilled at meditation, witnessing their thoughts and emotions silently for hours on end, can lose all ability to pay attention in a charged situation.

Remember, paying attention to feelings is not the same as expressing, exaggerating, or acting out. All it requires is a gentle focus, a turning toward what's already present. As you begin this practice, what may be present most often is a lack of feeling—in other words, a shutdown. Shutdowns aren't just big and dramatic; they are also small, everyday events. On any given day, the first shutdowns may happen even before you open your eyes.

I don't want to go to work. Who's making so much noise? The damn cat's in the way.

No matter how seemingly insignificant, thoughts such as these are often initial signs that you're fleeing the moment rather than opening to it. If you haven't yet found any tension in your body, they provide a reminder that it's time to look. The sooner you look for these shutdowns, the easier it is to reopen. That's why even just the hint of a shutdown is worthy of your complete attention.

I can't stand this traffic. My desk is a mess. Why'd she give me that dirty look?

Think of someone or something that's really been bothering you lately. Just for a while, no matter how unpleasant, let yourself dwell on this subject. Let all the frustration it induces arise without opposition. This will create an intentional shutdown. Now, turn your attention to your body. Where is the shutdown located? You might find a throbbing temple, a knitted brow, or a clenched jaw. You might find a tightened throat, a pounding heart, or a knot in the pit of your stomach. What one area draws your focus most acutely?

Once you've recognized the shutdown's primary location, keep your attention focused right on that spot. Don't try to understand what's happening there, or why it's happening. Don't judge it in any way, or attempt to change it or make it go away. Don't even try to describe it, or to distinguish whether it's mostly physical or emotional. Simply keep your attention on whatever arises. Invite it to express itself fully. Let go of any expectations about what's supposed to happen, or how. Trust that everything that transpires will be just right.

If your mind wanders during this process, gently bring it back. If you find your attention drifting toward the bothersome issue itself, return it to the sensations of your physical shutdown only. If the sensations begin to move, move your attention right along with them. If you see colors or images in your mind's eye, invite them to manifest fully as well. Make sure not to *urge* anything forth, or to become lost in what does come forth. Just continue to keep a close but relaxed watch, welcoming all that you experience and feel.

Strange as it may seem, this consistent and receptive awareness is all that's necessary for a shutdown to ease. Watch how long it takes. If you weren't already shut down before beginning the exercise, it might only be a few moments. At most it shouldn't be more than a minute.

The same tensions you just felt will likely occur whenever you're closed. Depending on the circumstance, they may occur alone or in varying combinations. A definite few, however, will show up more often than the rest. This is your shutdown pattern. It's unique to you. Learning your own patterns is a key part of becoming more open, not just to feelings but also to love. When you're closed, access to both is restricted. When you're open they can both flow freely.

Over the next few days, see if you can spot your shutdowns whenever they happen. Whether they're large or small, pay attention to them just as you did in this exercise. You can do this when alone or right in the thick of things. Soon, your own shutdown pattern will become clear. This will allow you to find it quickly. It will also enable you to recognize your shutdowns in the early stages, before they really take hold.

While it's relatively easy to spot and experience shutdowns, since they create specific physical sensations, the state of openness is a little more subtle. You can't point to it, and it exists in varying degrees. The absence of a shutdown indicates a certain amount of openness, but it may only be slight.

To understand openness more clearly, imagine yourself in the pouring rain without an umbrella. If you're on your way to an important meeting and can't get wet, the rain is a bona fide crisis. If you're headed nowhere special but would rather stay dry, the rain is a minor nuisance. If it's a warm summer day and you enjoy the cool cascade of drops, the rain is mostly welcome. And if you're delighted by the downpour, soaking it up in appreciation, the rain is positively cherished.

As you can gather, each of these instances represents a spot along the spectrum of openness, heading from least to most. Rain, of course, is what happens to you in any particular moment, and your ultimate goal is to cherish *whatever* that moment brings. This includes tragedies as well as triumphs, problems as well as solutions, joys as well as sorrows.

When you can soak up every single moment just as it is, without needing or expecting it to be different, then you've opened all the way. Such openness suffuses body, mind, and heart. It develops gradually, and can't be rushed. As you make your way through each of the Invitations, this openness will begin to happen naturally and without direct effort. Paying attention to your shutdowns is the all-important first step.

BODY LANGUAGE

Feelings, just like shutdowns,

are physical.

In the previous exercise, did you notice what happened after your shutdown eased? Most likely it didn't yield to tranquility. Since shutdowns are your attempts to keep from feeling, easing them enables emotion to flow. That means you probably began feeling some emotions, whether in the same place as your shutdown or somewhere else. Perhaps, if you kept paying attention, these emotions went on to crest and subside.

Whether we're aware of them or not, feelings always arise in our bodies. We feel them in our gut, chest, groin, throat, face, and even fingers and toes. Different feelings arise in different places. No two people feel things in the same exact place or in the same exact way.

Many people, over time, have lost their innate ability to locate a feeling physically. They may report, for instance, that a sense of frustration resides in their "brain." But brains have no ability for sensation. These people may instead be referring to a headache or a neck strain, or to a disturbance in their concentration.

If pinpointing the location of feelings is difficult for you, all that's needed is a little reorientation. Think of something that makes you glad, and then notice exactly where the gladness resides. Do the same with sadness, fear, anger, and regret. You may find that a feeling resonates throughout your body, or that it moves around from place to place. Such variations occur between people, and often in the same person depending upon the situation.

Once you are able to locate emotions independent from daily life, you can then do the same in the throes of it. Whenever a feeling arises, ask yourself where it is manifesting in your body. Pay attention gently until the answer comes. As soon as you know where a feeling lives, see if you can discern what the feeling is. With many emotions that's pretty easy, but others are harder to identify. If you feel an emotion but can't identify it, don't get stuck searching for a name. Instead, just describe what the physical sensations feel like. Usually, after a brief description, its essence becomes readily apparent.

Say you're talking with a friend, feeling calm and untroubled, then suddenly you experience a little tightness in your throat. It's not the kind of pain that indicates an ailment, so you wonder if it means you're emotionally upset. While continuing the conversation, you bring your attention to the tightness and keep it there. Is it fear? Anger? You're not sure yet, and you don't want to constrict your attention by straining to find the right label. So instead, you stay patiently with the tightness and silently note its characteristics. It feels hot, small, and pinched. There's also a slight throb to it. After just a few moments of attention and description, suddenly the tightness is gone. Rather than an emotion that needed further exploration, it was nothing more than a passing sensation.

Let's repeat the same example again, but begin it differently. Say that in the middle of the conversation with your friend you experience a shutdown. You know it's a shutdown because by now you're familiar with your pattern—pressure at the temples and grinding teeth. The shutdown lets you know for sure that there's an emotion involved, so you pay attention until it eases. In its wake comes the tightness in your throat. Now you place your attention there, but the emotion isn't immediately clear. So you keep paying attention to the tightness and note its characteristics. This time, the tightness doesn't go away. With a little time, though, it begins to shift. It moves into your face. There's a flush in your cheeks and you feel a little teary. All on its own, the sensation becomes an easily recognizable sadness.

If a sensation has emotional content, attention and description will almost always cause this kind of shift. This happens because the emotion *wants* to be understood. Your focus creates the time and space for it to communicate. In some cases the communication will come quickly, while in others it may take a long time. Continuing to pay gentle attention will allow an emotion to clarify as quickly as possible. Trying to force a premature sense of clarity will only prolong the process.

The quality of gentle, caring attention, as we've seen, will both ease your shutdowns and permit your emotions to reveal themselves. You may wonder why this quality is so powerful. There are four reasons. First, it attunes you to the language of your body. Second, it brings you home to the present. Third, it increases your openness. And fourth, it's one of the most fundamental ways to love yourself.

EMOTIONAL FLOW

Without interference, unpleasant feelings
depart as soon as possible.

*O*nce you've identified emotions in your body, and brought sustained attention to them, one further step is required. You need to greet them with real willingness. This means creating as much openness for your emotions as you're currently able.

Earlier, we used the metaphor of rain to understand the varying degrees of openness. Now, to help explain what openness means in this context, let's employ water again. Only this time, rather than using your imagination, perform the following experiment. As long as it's not a sweltering day, prepare a steamy hot shower or bath. Step in (without the book, of course). Once you're immersed, let the sensation of heat penetrate all the way through you. Bring your full consciousness to the endeavor. Dissolve yourself into the water as though you were actually melting.

In regard to your emotions, true openness feels almost exactly the same. It's as if you relax yourself to be two times bigger, then coax your feelings forward and encourage them to flow freely throughout all that extra space. While opening in this way to a pleasant emotion can provide a real treat, doing the same with an unpleasant one is much more challenging. Once you summon the necessary courage, however, the emotion does all the rest. Unimpeded, it never fails to move, shift, and change. It stays only as long as necessary, and eventually departs.

If a painful emotion persists or intensifies, and you're not exaggerating it in any way, that merely means there's much to be felt. And when you doubt the wisdom of remaining so open—perhaps to grief, shame, or gloom—remind yourself that the only alternative is shutting back down. In that case, as we discussed, the emotion is *forced* to stay put.

Opening to long-held emotions entails not just courage but also patience and will. As a general rule, the older emotions are the longer it takes for them to resolve. In some cases you may already be well aware of these emotions, working through them on your own or with a counselor. But just as often you will encounter them by accident.

Typically, a small matter produces a huge emotional response. At first you may be confused. You may exaggerate the matter to make sense of your response, or, on the other extreme, judge yourself for overreacting. But if you manage to let all that go and stay focused on the emotion itself, it often triggers associated memories. Suddenly you may be catapulted years backward, facing a reservoir of old feeling. When this happens it's best to proceed slowly, according to your own inner timetable. Almost always, however, the process is much easier than you first imagined. Often big releases happen right away, creating plenty of motivation to keep going.

What are you feeling right now? Where in your body are you feeling it? Keep your attention there for a few moments. If the emotion moves or changes, just follow wherever it leads. Do nothing except encourage the emotion to take all the space and time it needs. Whenever your mind roams, don't get discouraged. Instead, reel it in calmly as soon as you notice. If calm is all you're feeling, stay with that. If you feel nothing, find the greatest point of physical sensation and see whether anything else surfaces.

Keeping close company with raw emotion is an inherent skill that many of us have unlearned. Once relearned, it can be done under any circumstance, even amid chaos or when bombarded by the emotions of others. Sometimes, unwittingly, we bog down the process by talking excessively about our emotions or struggling to understand them. Both of these approaches, even if well meant, can divert our attention from the actual feelings themselves. We can easily become one step removed, attempting to dissect our feelings instead of fully allowing them.

Think of it this way—your feelings can't happen without you. Lack of direct attention, therefore, is a form of shutdown. This doesn't mean that you have to focus *only* on your feelings, or that you can't gain insight by discussing or analyzing them. What it does suggest, however, is that you need to stay aware of, and connected to, your ongoing emotional flow.

TRIGGERS

Certain events cause you to

shut down routinely.

Before moving on, let's review. The love we're discussing is different from love as commonly defined. It's not just about caring for others. It's not limited to our family, friends, school, or country. This love is universal. We can feel it at any time, toward any object, toward life itself, or even as just a basic attitude. Rather than creating this love, we access it. By opening to our feelings and allowing them to flow, we allow the love within us to flow as well.

Whenever we're not willing to feel, we shut down. But we can always reopen by paying close attention to our shutdowns in their precise physical locations. This attention not only causes our shutdowns to ease but also helps us to identify the feelings they've blocked. Once we know what a feeling is, and where in our body it resides, we can then embrace it fully. In doing so we provide all the time and space necessary for it to follow its natural course.

Even if you understand this, and are avidly learning to feel everything, your shutdowns will continue to occur. They may be caused by anything—a backache, a fight with a friend, car trouble, toxic waste. In time, as you watch when and how your shutdowns happen, you'll notice certain causes arising over and over. These are your triggers. It's important to know them well.

You may be particularly sensitive to the judgment of others, or financial pressure, or imperfections in your appearance. You may have a few intense triggers, or a whole host of minor ones. No matter how they show up, recognizing your triggers provides an essential aid in remaining open.

Do you already know most of your triggers? If so, take a moment to review them. See if you can discover any new ones. If you're not sure of your triggers, think about what makes you the most defensive or agitated. Consider the situations you try hardest to avoid. If you need a little extra help with trigger identification, ask the people closest to you. Our loved ones often have a clearer sense of our triggers than we do, since they witness our shutdowns with regularity.

Whenever you're triggered, the shutdown that inevitably ensues is particularly difficult to notice. It's a deeply unconscious reflex, usually followed by patterns of thought and behavior that keep your attention diverted. Immediately after a trigger has occurred, you may find yourself avoiding the feeling by trying to fix its cause. You may look for someone else to blame, or deny the whole issue entirely.

This is precisely why knowing your triggers is so vital. If an event has occurred that normally brings a shutdown about, view it as a call for special attention. Do so even if, especially if, it seems like nothing at all is amiss.

Let's say you're triggered by criticism, and some friends you're traveling with find fault with your driving. As a response you might ordinarily act out, telling them to mind their own business. Or perhaps you're prone to stewing silently, thinking of all *their* faults. Or maybe you'd pretend nothing is wrong, make a joke or change the subject, then wonder why the air is suddenly filled with tension. All of these reactions lack any awareness that a shutdown has occurred, or that an emotion is going unfelt.

So now, let's play it back differently. The passengers criticize your driving. Since you know criticism is one of your triggers, you suspect triggering may have occurred. Instead of reacting out of habit, you pause and focus on your body. You look for the personal shutdown pattern that you've previously identified. Sure enough, your shoulders have crept up to your neck, and your heart is suddenly pounding. Therefore, you know it's time to reopen. You keep your attention on the shutdown until it eases, then locate and identify the emotions that follow. Whatever feelings arise, no matter how mild or intense, you welcome them. All of this can happen without the others knowing, or you can choose to let them in. It's even possible, with a lot of practice, to converse about something else during the entire process.

When you approach all your triggers in this way, there are many benefits.

You release even your most serious shutdowns as soon as possible. You stay open longer and with greater frequency. You access your true emotional flow, and create an environment in which love can flourish. Since you're freed from acting out, or unconsciously trying to avoid your emotions, the choices you make grow wiser and more fulfilling. You're able to communicate about emotions honestly and directly. Plus, the more all this happens, the more your triggers lose their power.

FOREMOST FEARS

However strong your will to feel,

some emotions may still deter you.

*W*hich emotions are you most afraid to feel? When accepting the First Invitation, there's no more important question. Maybe you're particularly afraid of such commonly avoided emotions as guilt and rage. Maybe you're averse to more unusual choices like pride or joy. Or, perhaps, you're most afraid of fear itself.

Asking yourself which emotions you're most afraid to feel is another way to bring full attention to shutdowns that have previously reigned. Just the recognition of these foremost fears can begin to break down even the most ingrained defenses. So relax. Ask yourself the question, and then see if the answer comes.

If it doesn't, bring to mind your biggest triggers. What emotions do they usually elicit, especially after the initial reaction passes? In the previous example about an aversion to criticism, anger might flash at first, but then give way to hurt or humiliation. How about in your case? Are any of your triggers related to your foremost fears? If not, or if you're uncertain, here's another way to explore.

Think of the worst things that ever happened to you, not according to anyone else, or to society as a whole, but in your own estimation. You might settle on illness, loss, or abuse. Rather than scanning your life history intensely, remain receptive and allow your selections to arise. When they have, take note of the emotions you felt most at those times.

Next, think of the worst things that might happen to you in the future, such as poverty, betrayal, or dependency. Make these selections in the same effortless manner. Take note, in addition, of the emotions you'd most likely feel if these events came to pass.

There's a good chance that the emotions associated with your past and imagined traumas are some of the ones you fear most. Having such foremost fears, of course, is in no way dishonorable. It's an inherent part of the human experience. Even when you've acquired great skill at feeling everything, you'll still almost certainly be challenged by one or more emotions. The difference is that by then you'll be up to the challenge. You'll meet it with resolve, relishing the chance to connect with your core.

PORTRAIT: THE GIFT OF

GREAT LOSS

*L*aura came to her session with me racked by indescribable pain. A week earlier, she'd lost her twin sister in a terrible car crash. Her breathing was shallow, her posture stiff, and her tone both bitter and skeptical. Barely able to function, as a last resort she decided to Live the Questions.*

She began by asking herself the first question—"What is happening right now?" In doing so, she paid specific attention to her body, and to any sensations and emotions that arose there.

"I feel tired," she reported. "Tired down to my bones. I just want to stop, collapse, give up completely."

Then Laura asked herself the second question—"Can I be with it?" To be with something, as she'd learned, meant accepting with 100 percent of her being that it was actually happening. She didn't have to like it or give up her desire to change it, but rather just open to it completely.

Laura gave it a try. For a minute or so she just sat in stillness. Then she repeated the first question: "What is happening right now?"

"The tiredness is gone," she realized. "I feel . . . sadness. Rising up into my throat. And now fear. In my gut. I'm afraid if I feel all the sadness that's there, it'll destroy me. I won't be able to work, take care of my kid, anything."

Laura took a deep breath and attempted to "be with" the fear, to let it move through her at its own pace. A short while later it passed. Suddenly

Laura was sobbing, grieving, in a way she hadn't since the tragedy occurred. Many tears and tissues later, she confided the following.

"You know," she said. "I can do anger. I can do anxiety. But I never learned how to do sad. I mean, don't get me wrong—I've been a wreck since this whole thing happened. But that was different. Mostly I was trying to push it all away."

Laura had encountered a foremost fear, in this case sadness, and had opened to it valiantly. Even though the sadness remained, she was now present, fluid, and almost relaxed.

A few weeks later she had more to share. "I'm a lot better," she announced. "I miss my sister terribly, but I really can be with it now. And something else is happening, too. I feel like I'm getting to know myself in a different way. There's something about accepting all this sadness that isn't actually so sad. In a surprising way it's kind of, I don't know, satisfying."

* For a complete description of the Living the Questions process, especially helpful in working with foremost fears, please see my first book, *Unconditional Bliss*.

STORIES

Behind every shutdown there's
a rationale for not feeling.

Our most serious shutdowns can remain in place long after we've committed to letting them go. Usually, when this occurs, it's caused by the stories we tell ourselves about why we can't or shouldn't feel. Here are some of these common stories, each followed by a closer look at how they lead us astray.

IT WILL HURT TOO MUCH.

Ultimately, *not feeling* always hurts worse. Unfelt emotions fester inside us and create unconscious havoc. Beyond the feelings themselves, we suffer the effects physically, mentally, and spiritually. Many of our most important decisions, such as those involving our career path and romantic partner, can be skewed by stifled emotion. Everyday choices, as well, are often clouded by all we repress.

ONCE I OPEN THE FLOODGATES, THE FEELINGS WILL NEVER STOP.

Remember, *refusing* to feel is what causes unwanted emotions to overstay their welcome. The sooner we open the floodgates, the faster our feelings resolve. And often they only seem like a torrent because of the energy it takes to hold them back. Most emotions, once flowing, feel more tolerable than we ever anticipate.

I'M NOT THAT KIND OF PERSON.

All people need to feel. *How* we feel is what makes us unique. Some of us are prone to rollicking laughs and big sobs, while others just chuckle and tear up. Many stoic and impassive people, however, haven't yet allowed themselves to discover their true emotional nature.

I WON'T BE ABLE TO GET ANYTHING DONE.

Emotional presence is rarely debilitating. To the contrary, it makes us *more* effective. In addition to the personal energy and wisdom that result from such opening, we also gain access to the boundless energy of life itself. But there *are* certain times when life's duties make it inappropriate to feel fully. Most pressure-filled or adversarial situations, for example, would definitely fall into that category. That's why the First Invitation comes with no schedule. Whatever you can't feel now, you can always feel later.

I NEED TO BE STRONG, BOTH FOR MYSELF AND FOR THOSE WHO DEPEND ON ME.

Balling up for protection against waves of emotion is more weakness than strength. It renders you tight, depressed, and brittle. True strength comes from surfing those emotional waves, from riding them all the way to shore. Responding to life so authentically is the greatest gift you can give those around you. It will rub off on them whether or not they're aware of it. So, too, will all the love that accompanies such openness.

Are any of these stories yours? Are you aware of your own stories? If not, revisit your foremost fears and inquire—*Why am I so afraid of these emotions?*

What tales have I told myself about what will happen when I actually feel them?
Be patient. Let the answers take shape without strain.

When you've located some primary stories, use your understanding of the
First Invitation to defuse them. Here's an example. Suppose you have a foremost fear of feeling jealous, and that you're most triggered to shut down
whenever a close friend succeeds. A companion story might be *Feeling jealous
is pitiful and wrong. It will send my friends running for the hills.*

To defuse this story, you need to remember that feeling everything is not
the same as expressing everything. Certainly, you can feel overcome with jealousy and not share it with anyone. And even if you must share, the manner
and timing are completely up to you. But if your judgment about jealousy prevents you from feeling it, you'll just keep that jealousy on board. What's unfelt will infect your friendships anyway, probably more than you ever realize,
and more than would ever result from letting it flow.

For virtually every one of our shutdowns, we tell ourselves at least one
story. New stories arise all the time. The good news is that paying attention
to stories is no different than paying attention to shutdowns or triggers. The
skill is the same, and it improves the more you keep at it. Once you've brought
a story to full focus, you're then able to examine and release it. And every time
you do, you're that much more free to feel.

DIFFICULT PEOPLE

Those who bother you the most provide
a path to your unfelt emotions.

So far, we've explored the process of feeling everything as it relates to you individually. Yet none of us lives entirely alone. We encounter other people at home, work, play, and in the endless errands of daily life. Certain people, as we'll soon see, are the most challenging triggers of all.

The majority of your encounters with others—at the gas station, the store, the coffee shop—are likely to give you no pause. But then there are those occasional people who get under your skin. They may seem rude, selfish, or disrespectful. They may talk incessantly or give you the silent treatment. They may feign ignorance or think they know everything.

In terms of the First Invitation, these people are crucial for two reasons. First, they have an amazing capacity to shut you down, hard and fast. And second, just like all triggers, they point toward emotions that need to be felt.

To stay open, you must come to know the kinds of people, and the types of interactions, that get to you the most. Not only will this help you locate your shutdowns, but it will also point to the stories and foremost fears that are hardest to spot.

If you're especially aggravated by incompetent people, for example, it may point to a fear of things spinning out of control. The frustration you experience when things go awry could be part of a frequent shutdown. You may tell yourself a story about needing to hold it together at all costs, and therefore never allow yourself to feel an underlying helplessness.

Or, if indifferent people irritate you most, it may signify a fear of insignificance and neglect. You may tell yourself a story about the importance of people caring for one another, and never allow yourself to feel all alone.

Unfortunately, there's no simple formula for determining which unfelt emotions your response to a difficult person indicates. You may, for example, shut down in the presence of an arrogant person because you're unwilling to feel your own arrogance. But it is equally possible that such arrogance stirs unaccepted feelings of inferiority. As you observe yourself in relation to the difficult people in your life, the best way to assess whether you've made a true discovery is to see if it *feels* true. That means, no surprise, turning attention to your body and soliciting the answer there. It may come as a gut feeling, a vibration in your chest, or an overall sensation of knowing. A clear "yes" always resounds with conviction. A clear "no" either does the same, or else draws a complete blank. If you encounter something in between, you're probably still a little off target.

Once you become comfortable with this litmus test, exploring your interactions with difficult people provides an indispensable tool. And nowhere is this tool more valuable than with those closest to you. No matter how much you love your family and friends, things about them will always drive you crazy. This can often seem like a bother, or a burden, but it's actually an opportunity in disguise.

Take the time to make a complete list of everything that you can't stand about your loved ones. Don't edit or soften your judgments. Just for once, in service of self-discovery, let them all out full throttle. If you feel tentative or guilty about doing so, remember that this exercise is about learning to love and honor these people more. As your own hidden feelings about them come into focus, and you finally let yourself open to these feelings, the power behind your judgments will naturally decrease.

When you're done with this list of judgments, live with it for a while. Explore what it has to tell you about the feelings you're trying to avoid. You may be surprised by those feelings, as well as by the stories that stifle them.

Do you steer clear of a pushy sibling because you're not willing to feel overcome by anger? Is your unwillingness locked in place by a story that anger is wrong or unspiritual, or that family members should never fight? Or is that you wish you had the same strength of will, and haven't yet been able to accept your own meekness?

Do you tease a cheerful companion to stave off your own sadness? Is your refusal to feel that sadness tied to a story that privileged people shouldn't complain or hurt? Or is it that you're every bit as cheerful as your companion, but judge yourself undeserving to feel it?

Remember, how you respond to difficult people is entirely your own decision. In addition, when and for how long you investigate these relationships is also up to you. It may happen sporadically, in fits and starts, especially if you're taken aback by what's revealed.

Even when you've grown accustomed to such revelations, the emotions at the heart of them may take years to clear. The First Invitation, therefore, is a moment-by-moment proposition. It's only about one thing—finding what you haven't felt, and then feeling it whenever you can. In that quest, difficult people are your unknowing allies. When you approach them with this in mind, even at their most confounding, they often take on a precious glow.

ACCEPTING THE

FIRST INVITATION

To the best of my current and evolving ability, I resolve to:

- Pay attention whenever I shut down
- Experience emotions where they arise in my body
- Allow my feelings to come and go on their own
- Identify my primary triggers
- Face the emotions I fear most
- Discover the stories that keep me from feeling
- See difficult people as emotional signposts

THE SECOND INVITATION

Question Everything

To know is to be ignorant. Not to know

is the beginning of wisdom.

—J. KRISHNAMURTI

In the Second Invitation, love calls you to

reconsider all your beliefs about yourself,

others, and the world. Whenever you find

that a belief limits your openness,

you're then free to let it go.

"*L*ove is the answer"—it's a song, a bumper sticker, and a cliché. But in a way the message is misleading. It would be more accurate to proclaim that love is the question.

An answer is closed. It means that the investigation has been finished, that all discoveries have been made. When you've found the answer, you look no further.

Questioning, like love, spurs you to grow and expand. Rather than just believing what you've been taught or told, you come to prize the capacity to think on your own. What's true becomes highly personal, continually in flux, and subject to frequent review. In questioning with such conviction you bring a constant vibrancy to your sense of self, to all aspects of life, and to every single moment.

For most of us, putting this into practice is more difficult than it sounds. From childhood we're trained not to question but to conclude. We spend years developing a concrete identity, and then construct a life to reinforce it. We choose partners, friends, and communities of people who share our beliefs. We avoid or even judge those who don't.

On the societal level, we affiliate ourselves by class, race, and ethnicity. Celebrating our uniqueness can create confidence and strength, but it can also breed a sense of superiority and a distrust of outsiders. When we set ourselves apart or others do it for us, stereotypes result. To thrive, stereotypes rely on the absence of firsthand knowledge. If we don't question such unfounded opinions and our own role in perpetuating them, discrimination can quickly follow.

On the spiritual level, where love is meant to flourish, religious institutions can act out just like people. At one point or another, almost all have committed massacres in the name of God. They've frequently turned on themselves as well, erupting in factional disputes for money, power, and ideological supremacy. All of this continues today, with no tradition entirely immune. Such clashes are customarily fueled by a fierce resistance to questioning. As individuals, we're often forced to choose between loyalty and inquiry. When we hold back our questions in the name of devotion, transgressions frequently result. And just as frequently, if we do question religious authority, we soon find ourselves outside the fold.

Self-righteousness can also tempt those of us who follow a noninstitutional path. Even in the most alternative spiritual groups, disputes often arise over the slightest differences. And, perhaps just as often, members bond together to malign everything mainstream.

The Second Invitation, therefore, asks you to conduct a candid search for all your unexamined or divisive beliefs. To do so means revisiting everything you know. It requires you to shatter your frame of reference, and to step through it into virgin territory.

To begin, let's look at how your frame of reference formed in the first place. The initial element was heredity, which determined such basic characteristics as your body type and personality. This happened, of course, without any of your involvement or control. Next came your early environment, upbringing, and education, also all out of your control. By the time you graduated from grade school, your core values and beliefs were well developed, and very little of that development happened by choice. Free will played a part, certainly, but no greater than the role of chance. Whether you're Democrat or Republican, devout or atheist, sports fan or opera buff, these preferences have been shaped largely by circumstance. And even when you evolve later in life, or make sudden transformations, such seemingly autonomous changes rely on traits instilled long ago.

None of this is a problem—unless you forget it. Forgetting your circumstantial nature allows you to assume that your worldview is entirely self-developed, that it's entirely right or complete, when in actuality it can only be one single fragment of a vast, interrelated whole.

Does this mean that living in accord with love requires you to abandon your beliefs, opinions, and tastes? Of course not. But it encourages you to keep exploring, reconsidering, embracing whatever you discover and any shifts in perspective that may result.

Imagine that there's a wolf, bounding through the woods. It's strong, sleek, magnificent. To the naturalist this wolf is precious, one of God's hallowed creatures. To a hunter, this same wolf is a target, the source of sport and possibly a fur coat. To a scientist, the wolf is an object for dispassionate study. And to the nearby sheep rancher, whose herd has been slowly decimated, the wolf spells financial collapse.

The wolf, it's obvious, is all those things and none of them. The naturalist, hunter, scientist, and rancher each have a clear point of view. When they find themselves in disagreement, they can either take sides and vilify one another, or they can seek mutual understanding and common ground. They can choose to open or close, to question or answer.

While opening yourself to love makes you a more loving person, it doesn't preclude the possibility of disputes. It doesn't mean that simple solutions are always possible, or that there's always a happily ever after. But in accepting the Second Invitation, you minimize any unnecessary harm that your own viewpoint may cause. To do so, you must perform a courageous uprooting of any snap judgments, inherited stances, and absolute allegiances. Without abandoning your own interests, you're called upon to inquire first and decide later, much later. Actually, the most loving approach is not to take sides in any dispute until you can first understand and restate the opposing position with complete accuracy.

This is a tall order, especially when passions flare, yet love asks for nothing less. In fact, it compels you to go even further. Fully accepting the Second Invitation means not just asking questions, but instead *becoming* one. Only when your entire life is founded upon exploration, only when you're as comfortable in mystery as you are in certainty, only when you can open to new and differing points of view with the ease and constancy of breathing—only then will you have met love's challenge.

ILLUMINATING THE
SECOND INVITATION

Often that which is true will appear false, and that which

is certain, doubtful . . . there is scarcely a single truth of

which we can have complete knowledge.

—ST. JOHN OF THE CROSS

WHO AM I?

Questioning your everyday identity can
lead to a richer sense of self.

*W*ho are you? Or, more precisely, what makes you who you are? Is it your body and mind? Is it the work you do? The roles you play in family and society? How you feel and act? Your personality? Your soul? All of that or something else entirely?

These are the kinds of questions that often confound us as adolescents. Then, when we're older and busier, they fall by the wayside. But the moment we stop asking them, something vital inside us begins to die.

Many of us reawaken this type of questioning at a more sophisticated level when life doesn't meet our expectations. It may happen in church, during recovery, through meditation or other forms of spiritual exploration. If we're lucky, however, no single satisfactory answer will come. It's not much more enlightened to define oneself as an addict than a skateboarder, or as a child of God than a Mets fan. Any such definition is confining, incomplete, and exactly what gets in love's way.

The truth, as seen through the eyes of love, is that every single one of us is a unique and particular expression of the infinite. You'd be astounded, dumbstruck, to grasp the whole of what you are. The key to discovering this vastness is to question your own identity with diligence. This practice is similar, and builds upon, the attention required for opening to emotions.

To get the process started, take another look at the first paragraph above and search for as complete an answer as possible to the question "Who are you?" Begin by writing the phrase "I am" and then complete it with whatever pops into your mind. Do this over and over, perhaps a dozen or even twenty times. For example: *I am a (gender); I am a (nationality); I am a (religion/ atheist/agnostic)*. As you continue, make sure to include your various roles and responsibilities. *I am an executive. I am a soccer coach. I am a parent*. Before wrapping up, add some descriptions of your personality. *I am funny. I am smart. I am impatient. I am romantic.*

Now that your list is done, read your answers out loud. After each one, take a long pause. Notice the feelings and thoughts that arise with this particular identification. Let's say you've just pronounced, "I am a parent." At first you might feel a wave of love toward your family. Then you might feel some of the stress and overwhelm that parenting often brings. You might start to get angry at the lack of affordable childcare in your area, or wonder how you're ever going to save enough for the college fund.

By performing this exercise, you can quickly see how much energy and investment your sense of identity consumes. This is natural, unavoidable, but it's not the whole story. Now read the list out loud again, only this time insert the word "not" into each sentence (*I am not an executive, I am not a soccer coach, I am not funny*, etc.). Imagine, just for a moment, that all these renunciations are true. This gives you a chance to peel off layer after layer of everyday identity, and to see what, if anything, remains.

For some people, imagining themselves shorn of all roles and characteristics is frightening. For others it's a taste of freedom. How does it feel to you? Can you experience the part of you that exists beyond every item on your list?

If so, you've touched the region of your consciousness where love lives. It's through this formlessness that all things are connected, that we're all one. If you haven't yet been able to access it, try the final piece of the exercise. On a new sheet of paper, in large letters, write only the words "I Am." Repeat the words out loud, boldly, and let their evocation of pure being resonate within you.

If you're like most of us, such resonance is all too fleeting. Your sense of self feels threatened in the wings, and quickly resumes center stage. Its power to do so has developed over your whole lifetime. The goal of questioning is not to vanquish it, but to bring more of you into the limelight. The more you arrive, the brighter you shine.

IS THAT A FACT?

Your beliefs about yourself may be
outdated or inaccurate.

*A*re you tall or short? Thin or fat? Smart or slow? Attractive or plain? More important, how do you know? By comparison? Because you've heard it all your life? Would the answers change if you lived in a different family? A different culture? A different era?

Think of a personal quality that you've never really questioned. Maybe you've always been outgoing, gentle, or willful. Try to locate the earliest memories in which this quality played a part, and in which you began to incorporate it into your self-image. Did something happen at home, in the classroom, or on the playground? Chart the course of that quality from those first formative moments through the years that followed, noting any special occurrences that seemed to accentuate it. Did you get positive feedback for this quality in high school or college? Did it help you in your first few jobs?

Next, do the same for a quality that you've always *lacked*. Perhaps you've never been very quick-witted, graceful, or mechanically inclined. See if you can remember the first time you felt this quality's absence, and then any key experiences that intensified it.

As both of these searches make clear, self-perceptions arise out of the context and events of our upbringing. Over time, they become deeply ingrained. Often, when circumstances change, perceptions remain stubbornly fixed. Many slender adults, for example, still feel like the overweight children they used to be. Many rich people can never quite feel secure after their impoverished beginnings, and many overachievers continually compensate for being devalued early on.

Sometimes, the opposite occurs. If people struggle to replace one personal attribute with another, their whole identity may hinge upon this transformation. A previously fat person may become obsessed with thinness, a previously poor person with wealth, and a previously unappreciated person with continual acclaim. This type of overidentification with one particular trait can seriously skew a person's self-perception.

What about you? Are there parts of your own self-perception that have outlived their validity? Are there parts of you that go unseen or get distorted by your need to view yourself in one particular way?

It's not hard to grasp that many of the traits we take for granted about ourselves aren't actually givens but instead beliefs. What's challenging, on the other hand, is eluding the unwanted impact of those beliefs. The most common approaches to doing so involve replacing harmful beliefs with constructive ones. This might involve self-esteem–building activities or affirmations. If you see yourself as a timid person and want to be more powerful, for instance, you might be instructed to begin each morning with the phrase "I am strong, clear, and assertive in all my endeavors."

Almost anyone who's tried such approaches can attest to their great difficulty. As resistant as they are to change, beliefs are also highly sensitive to outside feedback. On occasion, even when we're riding high, just the slightest critical comment can give renewed strength to a negative belief we've supposedly overcome. Likewise, beliefs are also subject to our own shifts in mood. One bad day, for instance, can sometimes void months of increased self-worth.

The reason for pointing all this out is that the Second Invitation takes a completely different tack. It does not suggest that you try to like yourself one bit more or favor certain types of beliefs over others. Rather, it encourages you to recognize the tendency for all beliefs to be unreliable, and to question them with equal fervor.

Any belief, if held too tightly, can limit your ability to open. It can have the same effect as an emotional shutdown, cutting you off from yourself and the present moment. That's why investigating your beliefs about yourself is so important. It helps you to set those beliefs aside periodically, to see past them when necessary, to glimpse possibilities you might otherwise never encounter. Often, such an expansion of your perspective creates a thrilling surge of love. More than just self-esteem, this love is bigger than any single self. It connects you to that place in your heart where all beings dwell, and where there's unity beyond belief.

SHADES OF GRAY

When it comes to judging your own character,

no trait is all good or bad.

One way to break through the limits of self-perception is by investigating the value judgments that accompany them. Value judgments are beliefs that pertain specifically to worth. They're about right and wrong, good and bad. With that in mind, let's expand the list of key personal qualities you made earlier, such as *I am funny, I am smart,* and *I am impatient.* Include a wider variety of qualities this time, everything from *I am aggressive,* if applicable, to *I am a gossip* to *I am good with my hands.* When the list includes at least ten qualities, spend a moment with each to see whether you view it as mostly positive or negative.

Wherever you've assessed an item as positive, give a careful explanation why. For each quality, try to determine how and when your evaluation of it developed. Notice whether each belief is strong or a little shaky.

If you listed *I am supportive,* for example, you might point out that offering help to others makes for great friendships and is usually returned in kind. Maybe you remember an early incident at summer camp when an especially supportive bunkmate made a great impression on you. Yet perhaps you've been highly critical of others lately, and are wondering whether your helpfulness has waned.

Next, explore whether that same aspect of yourself could be seen as negative. Are there times when it's too much? When it gets in the way? Are there others who might think so even if you don't? What, in their own history and character, might lead them to take that view?

Keeping with our example, you might find on occasion that your support of others feels smothering to those it's intended to benefit. You might also conclude that it can be a smokescreen to keep you from focusing on your own needs. In addition, you might notice that certain friends respond harshly even to your most nonsmothering aid because they don't really feel deserving. In their case, due to their beliefs, offers of support only stir up shame.

Now let's continue. Wherever you've assessed an item as negative, go through the same analysis. What led to this evaluation? Does it ever waver? Are there situations in which this same part of you might be an asset? Or where it might even become essential? Would any people who know you agree? Would something in their own makeup influence the answer?

Whether negative or positive, as this exercise helps demonstrate, all value judgments about yourself are truly relative. Negative value judgments, obviously, have a great capacity to shut you down. But positive value judgments can also be limiting. As long as you perceive yourself through a good/bad or right/wrong lens, you can't possibly view the whole picture. Even if you judge yourself as all good, for example, absolutely brimming with wisdom and kindness, what happens at those inevitable times when you aren't?

Whenever a personal value judgment arises, it's tempting to judge yourself for that as well. Instead, however, you can gently question—*Is this the complete story? Am I leaving something out?* When you ask these kinds of questions with consistency, your value judgments soon begin to diminish. You see yourself much more clearly. Rather than straining toward ideals, you find yourself easing toward love.

VANTAGE POINTS

A worldview is the outgrowth

of circumstance.

How you see the world around you is every bit as subjective as the way you view yourself. Perhaps even more so, since you likely spend far less time examining it. Your gut reactions—to other people, situations, and world events—are based upon a host of circumstances uniquely your own. From these gut reactions flow the opinions and values that make up your vantage point.

Why do you love a certain song and revile another? Why does a popular coworker rub you the wrong way? What's behind your views on taxes, drugs, immigration? If you don't care about those issues, what leads you to disregard them?

To ask these questions, as you may have gathered by now, is more about gaining awareness than seeking definitive answers. It's another way to jar you loose from your habitual take on things, and from the conviction that any particular position exists independent of those espousing it.

Pick a topic you feel strongly about. Articulate your opinion on it with full force. Now ask yourself, *Would I be likely to have the same opinion if I were an oil baron in Texas? A waitress in Detroit? A beggar in Bombay? What if I were locked away in prison? Terminally ill? Or the victim of a violent crime?*

If shifting situations in this manner might change your opinion, what does that tell you? Can a point of view that's determined largely by fate ever be absolutely correct?

Many rational-minded people, when confronted with the subjectivity of belief, point to science as a way out. They rely upon the scientific method to separate unreliable personal perspectives from verifiable "proof." Yet the best scientists understand how each generation's theories are shaped by the prevailing culture, and how those theories evolve constantly over time. The worst mistake a scientist can make, no matter the discipline, is to consider any theory beyond review.

Many devout people, when invited to question everything, sense a challenge to the moral authority set forth by their god. The idea that there's no best way to see things, that there's no fixed right and wrong, can seem to throw the whole world into disarray. Like it or not, however, such disarray is a part of life. The dozens of conflicting groups within every organized religion provide a potent example. Since no divine text is without multiple interpretations, all of us are left, in the end, to make our own judgment calls.

Contrary to first impressions, then, the Second Invitation harmonizes with both science and spirit. It unites the two approaches by casting aside all filters that limit our perceptive capacity. Its call to constant questioning is what keeps us alive, awake, able to nurture both our understanding and awe.

STRETCHING

It takes practice to acquire

a fluid perspective.

*W*hen our muscles are stiff, or display a limited range of motion, naturally we stretch them. A similar stretching is required to keep our viewpoints limber. Purposely stretching our viewpoints is what renders the Second Invitation practical, relevant, more than just lofty words.

The following stretches are designed to be challenging, informative, and even fun. Do as many as you like, in any order and over whatever period of time feels right. Most important, take each stretch just to the point of healthy tension. Pushing too hard could cause you to recoil, and to question less instead of more.

Persona. Complete this sentence a number of times—I'm not the kind of person who . . ." Make your declarations specific, such as "hangs out in bars," "goes camping," or "chooses to be the center of attention." Then, as a brief experiment, do these very things. Monitor closely what it feels like. Think of it as research into different types of people and behavior. See if anything shifts within you.

Connection. Select someone in your work or social sphere with whom you find it hard to connect. Ask that person to lunch. Search out what you have in common, as well as what you don't. Try, when you've gone your separate ways, to see the world through your lunch mate's eyes.

Controversy. Pick a current issue—abortion, the death penalty, or something equally contentious. Make sure it's a subject about which you have a clear, strong view. Now, seek out someone with the opposing view and ask for a detailed explanation. Notice every time this explanation causes you to shut down emotionally. No matter what, keep listening. Avoid all interruptions and keep from silently planning your rebuttal. Then, repeat back the argument you've heard and check to see if you've done it justice.

Home Front. Perform this stretch with your partner, a close friend, or a family member. Focus on the most consistently problematic issue between the two of you—money, sex, judgment, jealousy, etc. Ask very directly what the other person feels in relation to this issue, and especially in regard to your own behavior. As in the last stretch, just listen, absorb, and make no effort to defend yourself. Next, repeat back what you've heard and make sure your understanding is accurate.

Field Trip. Visit a part of town that you usually don't go to and that's mainly populated by a race or class other than your own. Spend at least a few hours there, making sure to interact with a variety of residents—men, women, children, the elderly. Whenever you're about to approach someone, observe all your feelings and thoughts. Afterward, notice if the interaction has either confirmed or challenged any preexisting beliefs.

Worship Trip. Attend the weekly service of a faith other than your own. If anyone approaches you, say you're there to learn. If possible, have someone explain the subtleties of the service to you. Participate as much as you feel comfortable. Observe all your reactions without critiquing or censoring them. When the service ends, see if it has shifted anything in the way you view your own type of worship.

Adversaries. Find someone from an opposing political party. Ask for an unedited account of the things that make your own party the most loathsome. Listen carefully, noting all your triggers and shutdowns. Later, on your own, see if you can find any truth behind the generalizations.

Influence. List the people who've had the most influence on you— parents, teachers, friends, authors, and so on. Then take them out of the picture, one at a time, and imagine the ways in which you might have developed differently.

Subscription. For one year, subscribe to a magazine that supports something you detest. Read it cover to cover. If you don't want to support the cause with the cost of a subscription, use the library. Keep your reading exploratory, investigative, with a special emphasis toward finding any possible common ground.

Inventory. List ten of your strongest opinions about people and places, as well as about social, cultural, and political issues. Then make a candid assessment of how educated you really are on each topic. Are there any of these topics, in truth, about which you know very little? Would you be willing to admit it if there were, even just to yourself?

PORTRAIT: THE SHOCK

OF DISCOVERY

Margaret had always been shy and reserved. For the most part she considered that a virtue, an outgrowth of her commitment to humility. When beginning the "Persona" stretch from the previous Illumination, she completed the sentence, "I'm not the kind of person who . . ." with the phrase "hogs the spotlight and wears her heart on her sleeve."

Deciding to make the stretch a big one, Margaret auditioned for the chorus in the annual Christmas musical at a local community theater. Much to her dismay, she was offered a small speaking part instead. She took it, with some reservation, since rehearsals for the main cast required a lot of emotional sharing and exploration. Each time the cast got together, in fact, the director started things off with a round of personal check-ins. Margaret couldn't get by with just a few words, either, because if she tried to retreat into her shell the other cast members would pepper her with questions.

At first, participating at the theater filled Margaret with nothing but dread. It seemed like she spoke more in the first week, and to virtual strangers, than she had to her family over the past few months. Whether onstage or off, whether reciting lines or sharing something personal, "hogging the spotlight" would make Margaret feel dizzy, embarrassed, and even ashamed. She thought of quitting after almost every rehearsal, but that felt even worse than sticking it out.

Then, as opening night neared, Margaret noticed a big change. The personal check-ins no longer bothered her as much. She shared without any of her usual sweaty palms or heart palpitations, and actually began to look forward to it.

But the biggest change came in her listening. She noticed that she was increasingly eager to hear what the other cast members had to relate. She'd hang on their every word, nod with understanding, and offer special words of encouragement later.

The show debuted, and Margaret got through the run without making any gaffes. There was nothing particularly striking about her performance, except that she was the one doing it. Her husband and kids joked that she must have been possessed by an alien, and secretly it felt good to surprise them.

When her extended family got together for the holidays, Margarer enjoyed it more than ever before. She spoke a little more, too. A couple of times someone teased her about it, but mostly people didn't even notice. What Margaret noticed was how she listened differently, at least here and there, just as she had at rehearsals.

Driving to work the next morning it hit her—her shyness had always been tinged with *resentment*. She'd harbored a secret judgment about people who "wore their heart on their sleeve," a judgment based on anything but humility. As a result, she had listened to talkative people grudgingly, even bitterly. Stepping outside the comfort of her usual persona had caused her to see herself in a new and unflattering light.

When the shock of discovery wore off, as well as the guilt that accompanied it, Margaret was grateful for the whole experience. She had no desire to perform again, even though the theater asked. What she did desire was greater connection with the people who mattered most to her. To create that, she realized, would require more genuine sharing *and* listening. Since then she's done a lot better in this regard, but still sees a long road ahead.

WHY DO I WANT
WHAT I WANT?

No one is immune from

media manipulation.

*T*he opposite of stretching your viewpoint is tightening it. Such tightening can happen without your involvement, knowledge, or approval. This is often the effect of mainstream media and advertising. No matter how savvy you are about its impact, no matter how mightily you strive to resist, media messages can penetrate your mind like the most contagious virus.

Such a topic may seem out of place in a spiritual book, and in one about love most of all. Yet it's impossible to question everything and at the same time ignore what continually bombards us. The source of that bombardment is quite narrow, since only a few corporations now own most of the media. With the incredible development of technology, these corporations and their partners can literally, and efficiently, program some of your deepest longings.

Recognizing the role of media and advertising in contemporary life is not the same as complaining about the evils of TV or Madison Avenue. It's not about right or wrong, good or bad, or about shoving the genie back into the bottle. Instead, becoming aware of the degree to which you're programmed is what allows you to call it into question.

The advertising industry has become eerily expert at determining exactly what makes you tick, and what makes you buy. This is true even if you think you're immune to its methods. There's no escape—from the billboards, the product placement, the catalogues, and the market segmentation that grows ever more refined.

What do you crave most—safety? Money? Acceptance? Freedom? Whatever your answer, that's where you're most vulnerable. Craving is a kind of emotional trigger. It can shut down anything that gets in its way, especially your dedication to questioning, and override it with manufactured desire.

If such manufactured desire led to any kind of lasting satisfaction, it would be possible to make a case for it. But instead, the opposite is true. The goal of the system is to create a consciousness of lack, of endless need, which in turn stimulates further consumption. Reality, once luminous and full of mystery, becomes ever more flat and commodified. No toy, no rush of adrenalin, no fleeting sense of power can hold a candle to a liberated life. What they can do is deprive you of the time and focus necessary to create that life.

Embracing the Second Invitation requires you to pay special attention to where and how you're most susceptible to manipulation. Here's a way to get started. As soon as the time is right, set down this book for a while. Watch TV for an hour or read a glossy magazine. Pay close attention to the ads and see if any get you to crave. If they do, just sit quietly for a moment. Open to your craving without judgment, but also without making plans to satisfy it. Notice what happens when you give it such free rein. Does it only continue to swell, or does it eventually crest and recede?

If none of the ads get you to crave, focus on your greatest area of vulnerability. See if you can design an imaginary ad that would succeed where the actual ones failed. Placing yourself in the role of advertiser, even just briefly, can teach you a lot about your susceptibility. Often, it can even help you to seriously reduce it.

Whenever you find yourself in the throes of craving, take a big step back from the sensation and ask yourself, *Why do I want what I want?* When the answer to this question reveals an implanted yearning, it's an opportunity to unclench, to let go, to remember that no matter how much you're surrounded by messages to the contrary, love is never bought and sold.

A DEEP BREATH

Thriving amid uncertainty requires

calm and patience.

Questioning everything kicks up a lot of dust. Things we assumed were true are suddenly doubtful. Beliefs we've clung to for security no longer provide any. It's possible, and even likely, to feel a little lost. If this happens to you, it's time to take a deep breath and relax. Accept the Second Invitation at your own pace. There's no need to pressure yourself. In fact, doing so will only cause you to shut down.

The importance of calm and patience is something to keep in mind throughout all the Invitations. Most challenges are akin to a big boulder that you must push up a mountain by sheer force of will. Getting through school, succeeding in a profession, raising a family—all these goals require consistent effort, even when you have little left to give. Opening to love, on the other hand, is the opposite. While it, too, is often a major challenge, you can't meet that challenge with exertion. You meet it, strangely enough, by relaxing.

Remember the metaphor of the rain, and how fully letting in each moment is like reveling in a downpour? Recall the exercise in your bath or shower, in which you dissolved into the heat as a model for creating emotional space?

Opening to love requires a similar orientation. Love never goes away. It's available even, and especially, when you're upset, frustrated, or confused. But when you strive for it, the resulting constriction only keeps love at bay.

The task, whenever you find yourself striving for love the most, is to stop trying altogether. On the surface, the idea of trying not to try can seem contradictory. It can also seem like defeat, like giving up on your quest altogether. In practice, however, it's exactly what frees love up, and frees you up to tap into love's flow. If you haven't experienced this already, your first taste of it will create a powerful "aha." Afterward, each successive opening will arrive with greater ease, and will often be longer lasting.

Questioning, when done in a relaxed manner, can be a great aid in prolonging this openness. But what does the relaxed form of questioning entail? It entails not just living with uncertainty but embracing it. It entails feeling entirely at home in the state of not knowing, and cultivating that state with regularity.

Try the following experiment to get your feet wet. Over the next few days, whenever someone seeks your opinion, pause for a good, long moment before responding. Instead of saying the first thing that comes to mind, allow other possible answers to arise. Let them commingle. Question them all with equal conviction, and avoid picking one over all the rest. Instead, let your final answer become more of an exploration than a pronouncement. If you're worried about how all this might appear, go ahead and explain what you're doing. If it's you who can't take the silence and indecision, locate the discomfort they elicit in your body and focus on opening to that.

Eventually, befriending uncertainty in this way leads to a new type of balance. This balance allows you to continue making difficult choices and taking decisive action, but without the false sense of assurance you may be used to. Though balancing decisiveness and doubt can seem a little awkward at the outset, this is where the first two Invitations work together. When you're able to feel everything, as well as question everything, it creates genuine flexibility. You can remain balanced *and* relaxed, flowing freely with life *and* love, even when events are at their most turbulent. The best course of action, in this state, frequently becomes obvious and effortless.

Imagine, like Margaret in the previous Portrait, that you found a flaw in one of your supposed strengths. Let's say, through questioning, you came to realize that your greatest acts of generosity often came with an unstated demand for payback. This realization might cause you to shut down, distrust your own motives, and refrain from extending yourself at all.

Feeling everything, in this case, might involve opening to waves of guilt, confusion, and insecurity. You might also encounter anger at yourself, and at a history of actions that you now deem hypocritical. For a time, you might even judge yourself as essentially stingy. Yet, after all that passed, you'd be able to see yourself as neither altogether generous nor stingy. You'd just be you, capable of a wide range of responses that sometimes contradict each other. Without needing to shoehorn yourself into an overly restrictive identity, you'd have all the room necessary to take both a figurative and literal deep breath. This, in turn, would help bring a relaxed, spacious, and loving perspective to what was previously such a loaded issue.

The next time you felt generosity stirring, it would be a wonderful opportunity to inquire, *Can I give freely in this case, or do I need anything in return?* Rather than trying to hash this out analytically, your openness would allow you to connect to your body, without stress or interference, and determine which approach actually *felt* the most authentic. Perhaps it would feel right to give without any conditions. Or perhaps, for the first time, you'd feel compelled to make some conditions clear *before* giving.

So far, we've been discussing how to prevent the Second Invitation from leaving you a little lost. But it can also take a different toll, leading you to question hypercritically or compulsively. You may begin to use the process of inquiry as a defense, a shield, hiding behind it to keep from fully taking part in the world. You'll know if this is occurring when there's a cynical edge to the way you question.

Such cynicism might arise, for example, if questioning a trusted leader revealed unacceptable behaviour. This might cause you not just to question similar leaders in the future, but also to become overly suspicious. You might make blanket statements such as "It doesn't matter who's in charge—they're all alike."

Blanket statements are a possible indication that you've been triggered. It's therefore important, when you catch yourself making them, to postpone further inquiry. More questions at this point would only set you at odds, with one part of you shutting yourself down, and another trying to pry yourself open.

The remedy for this predicament is the same as the last—embracing the First Invitation along with the Second, so as to pause, expand, and relax. In the wake of your commitment to feel everything, any lingering shutdowns would ease. You'd uncover whatever emotions had been provoked. In this case, you might feel hurt, abandoned, and betrayed by the fallen figure. Unfurling yourself as widely as possible, and letting all these feelings sweep through the resulting space, would restore you fully to the present moment. You'd be truly open, not just to the backlogged feelings but to love as well. Your cynicism, without anything left to fuel it, would then naturally begin to melt. In its absence your questioning would deepen. You'd be able to evaluate all leaders on their individual merits, with an agile and unfettered mind.

ACCEPTING THE
SECOND INVITATION

To the best of my current and evolving ability, I resolve to:

- Expand my self-definition

- Regard beliefs about myself with doubt

- Avoid one-sided judgments of my character

- Recognize the circumstantial nature of my opinions

- Stretch my perspective

- Counter the effects of media manipulation

- Relax into my new uncertainty

THE THIRD INVITATION

Resist Nothing

What you resist persists.

—ANONYMOUS

In the Third Invitation love calls you to embrace

all of reality just as it is. This embrace creates a

peaceful relationship with your thoughts, and lays

the groundwork for positive change.

When life doesn't meet our expectations, we resist. We complain, blame, or deny. We shrink from life or rail against it, as if reality were our greatest foe.

Resistance happens naturally. It even makes a certain kind of sense. After all, why settle for less than what we want? As we're about to see, however, resistance is the worst possible strategy for change. Whenever we refuse to embrace our circumstances, or those of the world at large, it only helps to lock them more tightly in place.

One widespread form of resistance is emotional shutdown, which the First Invitation, Feel Everything, covers in great detail. The First Invitation also covers the way we use certain thoughts, or misleading stories, to reinforce emotional shutdowns and convince ourselves that we'd be better off not feeling at all. But many thoughts are a form of resistance themselves. These thoughts are the main focus of the Third Invitation. Whether we're aware of it or not, mental resistance can pervade our every waking moment.

What, exactly, is mental resistance? It begins with a condemnation of whatever is happening in a given situation. This situation can either be outside us or within us. Either way the thought arises, *It shouldn't be this way,* regarding anything from the weather to child abuse to our own perceived shortcomings. From that first thought streams a whole host of related thoughts about precisely what is wrong, why it's wrong, and how it ought to be different.

Let's say, for example, that you drive over a pothole. Your first response may be one of surprise, frustration, or disgust. And then suddenly you find yourself thinking, *I shouldn't have to deal with this. Every day it's the same thing. Are they ever going to repair these streets? What's wrong with this city anyway? It's not like they don't tax me to death. So where does all the money go? Into people's pockets, that's where. There's so much corruption I can hardly stand it. Not just here but all over. It's naive trying to be a giving person when everyone else just wants to take.*

A resistant thought is a negative thought. Negative thoughts feed off each other, creating a mental shutdown. Even though it exists in the mind and not the body, a mental shutdown is similar to an emotional one. It cuts us off from the present moment, and from the natural flow of life's energy. More than that, it renders us unable to feel love or access its power.

Love, as by now you're familiar, is the universal force of openness and connection. It surrounds you at all times, and emanates outward from your own heart. But in order to be experienced, love must be *received*. When your mind is closed you're incapable of receiving. Love has no way to get in.

From love's perspective, reality can never be right or wrong. It's simply what is. Usually, the moment such words are uttered, a cry of protest goes up in response. "Are you saying child abuse isn't wrong?! That we should just accept it, along with all of life's other evils? How can that possibly be in the interest of love?"

The answer to these questions comes in the form of a paradox. You cannot change what you don't first accept. And this acceptance can't just be lip service, but instead must involve your whole being. Many have become familiar with this concept through twelve-step programs, which teach that to overcome an addiction one must first admit the depth and severity of the disease.

This unconditional acceptance is required not just to heal addiction, but also to resolve any internal or external problem. As long as you resist, you cannot see the problem fully and clearly. As long as you resist, you remain mired in negativity. As long as you resist, it's more than likely that your solution to the problem will end up perpetuating it in another form.

Perhaps you've experienced such a repetitive cycle in your relationships, running from clashes with one partner only to repeat them with the next. Perhaps you've encountered a similar cycle regarding a weight problem or career challenge, unable to transcend it no matter how hard you try. Each of these occurrences bears the mark of entrenched resistance. The will for success is present, but it's foiled by an inability to accept the current reality, and to let love do its work.

Pursuing change while locked in resistance is as frustrating as it is ineffective. It's like trying to relax while beating yourself up. Imagine struggling to get your town's potholes paved over with a bitter, negative attitude. Your rants at city hall would most likely alienate even the best possible allies. Your letters to the editor would most likely turn more people off than on. If you went door to door with a petition, many of those doors would most likely slam in your face.

In contrast, pursuing change with a mind that's completely open is enriching, exciting, freeing. Imagine the same pothole crusade once you've unclenched yourself. You wouldn't like the potholes one bit more, but rather than shutting down every time you saw one, instead you'd get fired up. Government officials, newspaper readers, and neighbors would all have the opportunity to feel your infectious enthusiasm. Whatever chance existed for them to come on board, your positive attitude would almost certainly increase it. If your campaign were met by significant opposition, you'd be able to make your case with the utmost conviction and clarity.

Every aspect of life is full of potholes. But resistance to those potholes can take you to far deeper and more damaging depths. When you learn to drive past those depths without falling in, your journeys become as satisfying as your destinations. Plus, you arrive in much better shape. And even if certain potholes still remain, despite your best efforts to get them filled, this merely provides another opportunity to recognize and release your resistance. Aligning with love, remember, is a gradual and lifelong endeavor.

In spite of all the benefits that come to those who resist nothing, many people have serious difficulty embracing the Third Invitation. They assert, with great passion, that indeed things *should* be different. "The rainforests should be saved." "People with AIDS should be cared for." "Drug dealers should be jailed." Closer to home, such beliefs gain even more passion. "My partner should stop insulting me." "My boss should appreciate my work." "My kids should obey."

A case could be made, of course, for all these positions. But that's really not the issue. The issue is only how we relate to what exists right now, and whether or not we allow resistance to sap our vital energy and cloud our vision.

"Of course I don't want that," you may counter. "But reality often does make me mad. And that feels like the right response. It doesn't always sap my energy. Sometimes it motivates me. I'd be a fool, a fake, to act mellow all the time."

If anger arises, by all means welcome it. To do otherwise would make it impossible to accept the First Invitation and feel everything. It would leave your anger to fester, turn inward, or to vent in unrelated situations. Feeling the anger, however, is not the same as giving credence to all the resistant thoughts it may elicit. Nor does it involve creating a rigid opinion out of those thoughts. Such a response would make it impossible to accept the Second Invitation and question everything.

A moment of passing anger, or judgment, is completely natural and of little concern. Frequent bouts of anger or judgment, on the other hand, are signs of a mental shutdown.

Accepting the Third Invitation means paying attention to your thoughts. It means learning to recognize recurring negative thoughts as signs of resistance. Once acutely aware of resistance, in yourself as well as others, you can see how easily it leads to inertia and suffering.

On the other hand, when you're willing to let your resistance go, your certainty about exactly how a situation must change goes right along with it. You're free to reopen your mind, to consider new possibilities. Sometimes this leads to a better solution, and other times to a complete reassessment of the problem.

Resistance puts us at odds with the world around us. In a nutshell, it creates enemies. This is true whether the enemy is yourself, another, a whole group, or any aspect of existence. All your life you've heard the dictum "Love your enemies." And why not? How liberating such a love would be. Yet to dictate it is one thing, to accomplish it another. Such a transformation can't come about through will or hard work. It has to feel right, real. That's what happens when you resist nothing.

ILLUMINATING THE

THIRD INVITATION

Everything we shut our eyes to, everything we run away from,

everything we deny, denigrate or despise, serves to defeat us in the end.

What seems nasty, painful, evil, can become a source of beauty,

joy and strength, if faced with an open mind.

—HENRY MILLER

BEGIN WITHIN

Reviewing your list of personal standards
highlights the resistance they can cause.

*W*here does your resistance thrive? What causes you to shut down mentally on a continual basis? What negative and depleting thoughts build upon themselves for long stretches of time before you even recognize them? Answering these questions with honesty is what allows you to accept the Third Invitation.

Begin within. Look for the things you like least about your personality. These are liable to include some of the same qualities you first judged as negative in Shades of Gray (page 54). Perhaps you think you're not smart enough, attractive enough, charming enough, or ambitious enough. Maybe you view yourself as too timid, too sensitive, too demanding, or too unfocused.

In each such instance, if it applies to you, there's a self-created standard you're not meeting. Corresponding standards to the last four judgments above might be *"People should conquer their fears"*; *"People should ignore what others think of them"*; *"People should be tolerant"*; *"People should be disciplined."*

If such standards are moral in nature, they might begin with *"Good people should . . ."* If achievement based, they might begin with *"Successful people should . . ."* If personal growth related, they might begin with *"Aware people should . . ."*

What are the main standards to which you hold yourself? Are they mostly about morals, success, growth, or a blend of all three? Stop reading for a few minutes and jot down your top ten standards. These aren't about how anyone else should behave, just you. Allow them to come forth unfiltered, from that part of you that's unapologetically stern and authoritative. Make sure the standards cover all aspects of life—work, play, love, family, friendship, health, and spirit. The following is a sample list to get you going.

> *I should work harder than everyone in my office.*
> *I should make more money than my parents.*
> *I should force myself to get out of the house every weekend.*
> *I should treat my partner with kindness and respect.*
> *I should make sure my partner does the same.*
> *I should stay up-to-date on my family members' lives.*
> *I should call my close friends weekly and see them at least monthly.*
> *I should be fit and active, exercising three or more times a week.*
> *I should let nothing get in the way of my spiritual growth.*
> *I should journal, meditate, and pray daily.*

Once you're done with your list, rank the items in terms of importance. Then rank them according to how of much a role they play in your everyday life. Now take a moment to digest all the information. Is any of it new to you?

Whenever you hold yourself to a standard and come up short, resistance may soon arise. This resistance usually takes the form of excessive self-criticism. Working off the sample list above, here are the types of thoughts that may result. *I'm not disciplined enough. I'm not wealthy enough. I'm boring. I'm selfish and mean. I'm a doormat. I let my family down. I'm a bad friend. I'm lazy. I let God down. I'm a bad person.* What's important to understand about these thoughts is that they're all vague value judgments. They create a negative and unloving internal environment. And, most important, they usually just reinforce the status quo or make things worse.

All self-criticism, of course, is not like this. It is possible to discover and accept a current shortcoming, map out a means of self-improvement, and then enthusiastically begin the process of change with an open mind and heart. If you're not sure whether an occurrence of your own self-criticism is resistant or not, here's an easy way to tell the difference. Resistant self-criticism brings you down, while resistance-free self-criticism lifts you up. When you're excited about changing something for the better, there's no reason to take another look. But when the way you are right now creates deep-seated frustration, or a sense of futility about the possibility of change, there's definitely resistance to explore.

Excessive and resistant self-criticism can easily become ingrained, automatic, and unconscious. This type of thought tends to run on its own track, devoted solely to negative self-assessment, and to providing an inexhaustible supply of answers to the question *What's wrong with me?* Such a debilitating Q&A often becomes the white noise behind all other thoughts, and the stress it creates is enormous.

As you finally begin paying attention, and survey all the stress up close, it can be a cause for great alarm. The frequency and intensity of your resistant self-criticism may seem overwhelming and unconquerable. It may feel like the one barrier to love that you just can't transcend. Fortunately, as we'll now see, that isn't the case.

THE POWER OF ACCEPTANCE

Resistant thoughts can't survive

without a fight.

*P*aying attention to resistant thoughts, and to the process of thinking as a whole, reveals new information. You come to see that in general there are two types of thoughts: the kind you will into existence, like those at work in creativity and problem solving, and the kind that just arise on their own. This second type of thought, to which resistance belongs, is what's happening in our minds most of the time.

Consider what goes on when you're driving, shopping, or reading a book and suddenly your concentration wanes. From out of nowhere comes one stray thought, then another, then another. They may be important or inconsequential. They may be connected or have little to do with one another. In mere moments your mind loses track of itself completely, travels all the way around the world and back.

From the standpoint of the Third Invitation this is not a problem or a weakness. Rather, it's just a part of the mind's nature. That's why you have so little control over it, and why efforts to combat resistant thoughts are rarely successful. If you try your hardest not to think resistant thoughts, it's almost impossible to succeed. Why? Because you don't create resistant thoughts in the first place—they arise spontaneously out of your unconscious. Therefore, you're not even responsible for having them. What you *are* responsible for is how you respond to them. And when you respond to a resistant thought by resisting it, you only add fuel to the fire. You waste valuable energy by trying to shield yourself from something that already exists, and by opposing life's natural flow.

This point is so important that it requires a little more explanation. Let's revisit the litany of vague value judgments from the previous Illumination. *I'm not disciplined enough. I'm not wealthy enough. I'm boring. I'm selfish and mean. I'm a doormat. I let my family down. I'm a bad friend. I'm lazy. I let God down. I'm a bad person.* These are all very resistant thoughts. You'd certainly be better off without them. And yet, you neither choose for them to arise nor have the power to squelch them if they do. Furthermore, you can't even banish them from this point forward. In fact, any attempt to do so would only prolong your mental shutdown and consequently banish love instead.

Without undue stress or struggle, however, you *can* stop any train of resistant thought from continuing. At the same time, and with the very same method, you can limit its reappearance in the future. To do so requires only one thing—meeting your resistant thoughts with acceptance.

Accepting resistant thoughts requires two things: first, becoming aware of them, and second, welcoming them completely. The process is no different from the way you learned to lean into difficult feelings when working with the First Invitation. You don't often make a conscious choice to feel lonely, for instance. But once you recognize that you *are* lonely, you then make that loneliness feel right at home. You give it all the time and space necessary to resolve, realizing that this will also bring about the fastest possible resolution. Likewise, you don't choose to think, *I'm a doormat.* But once you recognize that the thought is present, you greet it with warmth and appreciation. You do this even if the thought is troubling, and even if you don't really believe it.

Let's say you're in a meeting at work and a subject comes up about which you have lots to contribute. Instead of speaking up, however, you remain silent. And then comes the torrent of resistant thoughts. *Why didn't I say something? I've got a better perspective than anyone here. I'm afraid they'll shout me down, or criticize me. That's the way I always am. So tame, so pathetic. Successful people should conquer their fear. Successful people should ignore what other people think about them. This is exactly why I'm not successful. It's why I'll never be successful.*

Perhaps this uninvited torrent will continue for a long stretch before you become aware of it. With practice, however, your recognition will arrive much faster. Soon, just the quality of resistant thoughts will stand out immediately, drawing your attention like a clap of thunder. Whenever that recognition comes, your goal is to accept. Remember, this acceptance doesn't mean you have to like or believe any of these thoughts. It only means that you behold them in peace.

Accepting is a silent process, with no words to it, but transcribed into language it might come across like this—*Resistance . . . Hmmm . . . Thank you . . . Take your time, spread out, stay just as long as you like.* There will be ample opportunity later to find the bits of truth in your spontaneous reaction. There will also be chances to devise a better way of handling similar situations when they next occur. But first, before all that, you must set the stage with unqualified acceptance.

In the wake of such acceptance you relax. You separate from the thoughts and are less swayed by them. Often they come to seem like bad-tempered children, screaming bloody murder but really just needing some caring attention. Sometimes, for all their destructive force they can even seem comical, almost ridiculously over the top.

Perhaps this all seems counterintuitive. Perhaps you imagine that such a response will cause resistant thoughts to gain power, run rampant, and ruin everything. But here's the irony—they almost never do. Instead, with such a generous welcome, resistant thoughts back down and surrender their fight.

That is, of course, until the next resistant thought appears, which may only take a few moments. But these new resistant thoughts, when met with acceptance, will surrender in the very same way. Each time this occurs, it chisels a new crack in the wall of your resistance, enabling love to shine through, first in mere slivers but soon in great, all-enveloping shafts. In this transformed environment, resistant thoughts arise less and less. In their place come loving, compassionate thoughts. These positive thoughts, just like resistant ones, nourish each other and quickly proliferate. This happens even in the heat of the moment, all on its own, and without conscious intent or effort.

REFOCUSING

Harmful self-criticism can become

helpful observation.

Meeting resistant thoughts with acceptance allows you to soften and expand. It creates the space necessary for your perspective to broaden and your understanding to deepen. Refocusing is a helpful tool in this process.

To refocus means taking a big step back, and evaluating any difficult situation from a more objective distance. It means switching your awareness from what you think is wrong with a given situation toward a judgment-free observation. In the previous hypothetical work scenario, you were filled with self-critical resistance for not participating in the discussion. All your focus was on what you didn't do, what you should've done. Once you've recognized and accepted all those resistant thoughts, you can then refocus. Refocusing on what actually occurred might lead to the following observations. *I had something to contribute. I was afraid. My fear kept me from speaking up.*

Such a straightforward explanation is much easier to accept. It's stripped of negative descriptions like "pathetic." It's also free of damning conclusions like "I'll never be successful."

Refocusing resistant thought can help further acceptance in almost any situation. When you eat too much, your resistance may spin a tale of lifelong obesity and sloth. In response, you can refocus toward the specific lapse and any emotional shutdown that may have led to it. *I meant to have two bites. Instead I finished the whole thing. I'm not sure why, but I've certainly been stressed about money lately.*

When you blow up at a loved one, your resistance may exaggerate you into a complete brute. Refocusing, however, would tell a different story. *I snapped. I yelled. I said things I didn't mean because I was so angry and hurt.*

Pick an aspect of your life that routinely causes resistance. Bring to mind the most common resistant thoughts that occur, prior to any acceptance or refocusing. It's helpful to write these resistant thoughts down so you can see them clearly. You might decide to pick, for example, a lifelong problem with procrastination. Your written list of common resistant thoughts might include something like the following: *Here we go again. I never have what it takes to get things done. Other people don't seem to have this problem. They just deal with their own blocks and get on with it. I guess there's no way around it—I'm a failure. I should stop wishing for things to change because they won't. Obviously I don't deserve anything better.*

Once you've had a chance to review your written list of thoughts, then it's time to accept them. Acceptance, as we discussed, is nothing more than a willingness for these thoughts to exist. Since they already do, your acceptance brings you in line with reality. It means that even though the thoughts want to fight with you, you refuse to fight with them. Instead, you acknowledge them silently and calmly. *Whoa. That sure was a tirade. I hear you loud and clear.*

When you've accepted resistant thoughts fully, you'll notice a lack of negativity toward them. You may regard them neutrally, or possibly with feelings of disappointment, but no matter what, you won't be trying to will them away. This means you're ready to refocus, to step back from the thoughts and notice all the value judgments and damning conclusions involved. In the case of our example, such judgments and conclusions include: *I never have what it takes. I'm a failure. Things won't change. I don't deserve anything better.*

With all such judgments and conclusions clearly identified, you can then complete your refocusing. To do so, write out a simple evaluation of the situation that contains no resistance whatsoever. For our example, the evaluation would be something like: *I have a problem with procrastination. Since it's been going on for many years, and I haven't solved it yet, it might be time to get some help.*

The more willing you are to embrace reality in this way, the less problematic it seems. Soon it becomes a great relief to stop intensifying your resistance by fighting it. Your protective armoring begins to slide right off. You find yourself coming to appreciate the very same circumstances that were once unbearable, since they're the catalysts for your greatest growth. This growth, helped along by acceptance and refocusing, is what allows your love to grow as well.

INQUIRY

Questioning your core beliefs reduces

stubborn resistance.

The Third Invitation goes hand in hand with the Second. To resist nothing, it's often necessary to question everything. The babble of resistant thought that rages within us draws much of its power from our unexamined beliefs.

For an illustration, let's return to our previous example. The resistance that arose during the work meeting stemmed from a belief that overcoming fear with courage is necessary for success. It was the momentary lack of courage that led to the conclusion, *I'll never be successful.*

Now let's investigate that belief. Is it true that many successful people are courageous? By all accounts, yes. But is it true that *all* successful people are *always* courageous? Certainly not. Some successful people make it to the top primarily through heredity. Some are in the right place at the right time. Some worry excessively about what others think of them. And some struggle with persistent fear.

In certain cases courage is indeed the cornerstone of success. In your case, who knows? The belief behind your resistance, then, is at best only partially true. At worst it's totally false. Questioning that belief, and seeing through it, can melt resistance right in its tracks.

Each time you question the beliefs underlying your resistance, you get a little bit better at the practice. Soon it requires very little effort, and in time it becomes second nature.

Beneath most underlying beliefs, however, are even deeper convictions, ones that can take a little more digging to find. In our current example, it would be necessary not just to question your belief that courage is vital to success, but also to question why you value success in the first place. Such an examination might uncover the core beliefs *Success will make me happy* and *Success will allow me to do all the things I've always wanted*. But are these beliefs true? Is it equally possible that becoming more successful could make you miserable? Could all the pressure and responsibility become overwhelming? Could you end up with less free time rather than more? The answer to all these questions, of course, is *yes*. But will any of that actually happen? The truest response is *who knows?*

Revisit your list of top ten standards from the Begin Within section on page 79. For each standard, see if you can determine and then challenge one or more of its motivating core beliefs. The standard *I should always be nice*, for instance, might be motivated by a core belief that niceness is good. But is it *always* good? Aren't there situations when it's more important to be forceful and direct?

The standard *I should always work as hard as possible* might be motivated by a core belief that hard work produces the greatest success. But does it *always* do so? Don't some of the greatest inspirations come through imaginative play, or from musing idly on a beautiful day?

The standard *I should find and fix every personal flaw* might be motivated by the core belief that the goal of spiritual life is perfection. But is it the *only* goal? Isn't embracing *im*perfection also a part of spiritual life?

Sometimes we're so enmeshed with our core beliefs that it's not even possible to articulate them. If you find that's the case regarding what underlies any of your top ten standards, ask someone else to help you question and explore. An outside perspective can almost always bring your core beliefs to light. It can also help you assess how true those beliefs really are.

Subjecting your core beliefs to inquiry is like yanking the rug out from under resistance with one swift tug. Since you no longer always know what's right, your personal standards become more spacious and loving. You're able to accept yourself at what seems like your worst, which is what enables you to become your best.

PORTRAIT: WHAT IF
I'M REALLY A FRAUD?

*R*obert had spent the last twenty years developing his own consulting company. Incredibly successful, he and his staff of sixty provided accounting services for a number of leading corporations. Then he was asked to take on a project much bigger than ever before. A part of him wanted to turn it down, afraid of all the extra work and possible failure, but another part of him was thrilled, honored, and felt he owed it to his associates. After much wavering he decided to make the deal.

The months that followed brought a mounting sense of overwhelm. Robert regretted his decision. He felt the company was stretched beyond its capacity, and that its work was suffering. The client didn't seem to notice . . . yet.

Soon Robert wasn't sleeping. During most days he was uncharacteristically brittle and moody. He saw a psychiatrist who suggested medication for both depression and anxiety. Robert balked, wanting first to see if he could solve the problem himself.

He began by paying very close attention to his resistant thoughts. Their consistency and virulence caught him off guard. *You're such a disappointment, such a fraud. You don't deserve to run a company. Now everyone will finally find out. Your wife will leave you if she knows what's good for her. Anyone would.*

Robert tried to accept all these resistant thoughts one at a time whenever they came, but at first it was too hard. So instead he set out to refocus. With a more detached part of himself he outlined the situation: *It feels like I bit off more than I can chew. No one else seems worried about it, but I sense they will be soon. Experiencing all this pressure has brought up a lot of shame. I get the sense it taps into some childhood shame as well.*

Refocusing didn't cause the resistant thoughts to decrease, but it did give Robert a bit of distance from them. This allowed him to begin a serious inquiry. Right away he recognized an obvious internal standard—*I should not disappoint other people.* Probing beneath that standard he found a core belief—*Disappointing other people, or even just thinking that I've disappointed them, makes me a bad person.* And then, for all his success, Robert had to face an even more deeply rooted belief—*I am a bad person.*

This discovery was a real blow. With a lot of encouragement, Robert tried to accept the part of him that made such a brutal judgment. He brought as much tenderness and compassion to the effort as possible, but the resistance only diminished a little. It was then, aided by some coaching, that he took a dramatic step.

Until now, Robert had been hoping not to continue thinking all these critical thoughts. More than anything he wanted them gone. At this point, though, he decided to imagine that they were all true. For just a brief moment he began to consider—*What if I am a disappointment? What if I don't deserve all my success? What if I'm basically a bad person?*

Robert feared that this experiment would cause him to crumble, to lose it once and for all, but something very different happened. He felt only relief. Imagining himself beyond repair allowed him to let go, to give up the fight, to stop beating his head against a wall that would never crack. This didn't mean actually agreeing with the thoughts. Instead, it just meant accepting their content as well as their existence.

With that shift, the thoughts finally began to subside. In their place came sadness and vulnerability. These feelings had been there all along, of course, but now he was free to embrace them. In addition he could ask for help, letting key coworkers peek behind the veil of his authority. These coworkers, previously immobilized by the panic they silently sensed in him, were grateful to be called upon for support.

In time, the project became more manageable. Robert regained some of his strength and began sleeping again. His resistant thoughts, however, didn't magically disappear. In fact, from time to time they resurfaced in bursts. But with acceptance, refocusing, and inquiry, he now had a number of loving ways to respond to them. And just the ability to do so filled him with a new kind of self-respect.

WHAT IS

Accepting things just as they are

enables you to distinguish between

resistance and discernment.

Until now, in examining resistant thoughts and how to meet them with acceptance, our focus has been solely on you. It takes time, patience, and lots of attention to become skilled at recognizing and releasing resistance directed at yourself. Once you're accustomed to the basic process, however, you'll find that it works equally well with resistance directed toward others.

The best way to explore this outward resistance is to begin close to home, then gradually widen your circle of awareness. The first arena to consider is that of your friends and family. How do you view them, individually and together? How do they view you? How do you all communicate with one another, interact with one another? And what about any of that causes you to resist?

Upon close inspection, you'll likely find that these relationships are fraught with resistance. If at first it doesn't seem so, give yourself total permission to let your resistant thoughts appear. Then, think about the three or four closest people in your life, zeroing in on the most common sources of conflict between you. For each of these people, as many times as fits, complete the sentence "Sometimes I wish he/she would . . ." Do the same with the sentence "Sometimes I wish he/she would not . . ." Don't hold back your criticism, even if you find yourself shocked at its intensity or extent.

No matter how frequently you resist your family and friends, it's still possible to meet that resistance with acceptance. Resistant thoughts only appear one at a time, and can therefore be accepted one at a time. Remember, accepting resistant thoughts doesn't necessarily mean changing your opinion. Nor is it about whether your friends and family should or shouldn't change their behavior. Meeting resistance with acceptance is a way to open your mind, and then your heart. It's about remaining connected to yourself, and to others, even when it seems nearly impossible. It's about letting yourself experience love in every moment, and then sharing that love to make room for more.

In the beginning, even when you're clear about its purpose, accepting all your resistance toward others can occasionally prove exhausting or overwhelming. If it does, both refocusing and inquiry can help ease the way. Let's say, to demonstrate, that you're at lunch with a friend who's talking only about himself. You find yourself tuning out, and notice a flurry of resistant thoughts. *He hasn't asked me a single question. He doesn't really care about me at all. He should go into therapy. He should learn that he's not the center of the universe.*

Refocusing these thoughts might yield a sober, less emotionally charged assessment. *At the moment the conversation is lopsided. It seems to fit into a pattern. I notice it's making me angry.* Inquiring into these thoughts would reveal a number of dubious beliefs. How much does your friend really care about you? It's impossible to know. What effect would therapy have? It's impossible to know. Does he really think he's the center of the universe? Again, it's impossible to know.

Connected to all these questionable beliefs might be an external standard—*My friends should care about me as much as I care about them.* Just like the internal standards we discussed earlier, external standards, when seeming to go unmet, can lead to considerable resistance. Underneath this particular standard might lie the core belief that good friendships are equally balanced.

Continuing with your inquiry would allow you to challenge the universality of that core belief. Is equal balance *always* required? Can't the balance fluctuate from time to time? Don't some friends get very different things from one another? How is the balance calculated then? Aren't there some people inclined more to giving, and others more inclined to receiving? Such questions would help soften your certainty about the current situation. They would most likely mark the beginning of acceptance. And along with acceptance, just as likely, would come a much clearer understanding of the situation.

This friendship may have been stuck for awhile. It may not serve you anymore. You may, indeed, have a preference for continual reciprocity that can't be matched by this particular friend. On the other hand, one or both of you may be harboring unspoken issues that have colored your reactions to each other. Perhaps a heartfelt clearing of the air is what's needed to heal the rift.

The point here isn't that the friendship should continue or end. It's that while in resistance you can't really tell. You may, for example, unconsciously be using your philosophy of friendship as a way to avoid feelings of hurt. Your resistance would then keep you reactive and limit your options. But the moment you found it, and accepted it, you'd become free to make the most loving decision.

Once you develop the capacity to spot resistance and the avalanche of negative thought it unleashes, suddenly it can seem to be everywhere. At work, on the road, in the dentist's office and the grocery store, you come to see how your resistant thoughts are continually in the way. It may even start to seem that all reactions, all opinions, all critiques are similarly suspect. There's a key difference, though, between resistance and the quality of discernment.

Most of the time, resistance carries a "negative charge." A negative charge is a powerful feeling of internal tension. It's uncomfortable, bothersome, and sometimes downright intolerable. Discernment, by contrast, carries little or no charge. You may not enjoy a certain movie, not choose to live in a certain city, and not want to socialize with a certain neighbor. In these cases your assessment is calm and untroubled. You simply rely upon it to navigate through life.

But it's also possible that you *hate* the movie, *abhor* the city, and *despise* the neighbor. Strong positions like these are prone to carry an equally strong negative charge. The stronger the charge, the stronger the resistance. Wherever life troubles you most, your most powerful resistance is almost certain to dwell. Therefore, when making important decisions, one of the most valuable questions to ask is this—*Am I deciding out of resistance or acceptance?* If a negative charge is present, you're probably choosing out of resistance. If no negative charge is present, chances are you're exercising genuine discernment.

TAKING A STAND

When you no longer resist the world,

you're able to make it better.

Continuing to widen your circle of awareness brings you, eventually, to the news of the day. Whether you await it anxiously or do everything you can to avoid it, the world's turmoil still seeps into your mind. And with it can come more resistance.

After a news story about drunk drivers, you may denounce those with no restraint. After a story about lung cancer, you may curse the tobacco industry. After a story about child hunger, you may condemn our entire society. And once again, you may find yourself at odds with the Third Invitation.

If I'm supposed to accept everything that goes on in the world, remaining neutral and without a charge, then how can I ever take a strong stand? How can I ever be myself? People aren't all the same. We're not supposed to be the same. Conflict is what makes the world go 'round.

An objection such as this leads to a vital distinction. It's possible to take a stand, even passionately, with resistance or without. What makes the difference? It's entirely experiential, which means you can test it yourself.

The next time you hear a news story about terrorism, for example, pay specific attention to the quality of your thoughts. More than likely, they'll carry a very high negative charge. You might find yourself tense, fearful, raging, depressed, or some combination of all the above. A representative inner monologue may go something like this:

Why can't people just live in peace!? Will the cycle of violence ever end?! It's the innocent who always suffer. What if something happens to me, or my loved ones? I can't even stand the thought of it. I wish this whole thing would just go away.

If you find that your view is resistant, in this way or any other, that doesn't mean it's wrong or invalid. Rather, it's a call for the most spirited acceptance. To accept the world as it is means embracing cruelty, uncertainty, and even indiscriminate carnage. It bears repeating that such acceptance neither sanctions the current state of affairs nor precludes assertive action to change it. What it does do, however, is allow your own response the chance to be transformed. When listening to the same news story about terrorism, your inner monologue might now go something like this:

Why can't people just live in peace?! Will the cycle of violence ever end?! Wow, I didn't realize how much resistance I had about this. I feel waves of fear, and sadness. And I recognize a lot of standards and core beliefs at play. Like "I should be safe," "The world should be safe," "My country is good," "Terrorists are evil." Reflecting on these statements now, I can see how all of them may not always *be true. And how thinking they are would keep me resisting.*

After more time with these feelings and beliefs, your inner monologue might conclude on quite a different note:

I still feel fear. I still feel sadness. Both for myself and the whole world. But I also feel compassion, and love for everyone who's affected. Regardless of my beliefs, mostly I'd like to help. I'm not an expert, and I don't know how to solve such a huge problem. I want to do my part, though, no matter how small it may be, in the effort to create lasting security.

When strong points of view are unhindered by resistance, like the one above, they tend to be fluid and rousing. In contrast to the resistant variety, these viewpoints carry a *positive* charge. They turn you on, light you up, foster loving and lasting empowerment. Plus, they make you better able to communicate your view without causing similar resistance in others.

The above example, of course, is necessarily brief and general. It may not represent your own feelings and beliefs about terrorism at all. It may also seem to resolve a little more quickly and neatly than many types of real-life resistance. Using it as a framework, however, can help get your own investigation started.

Choose another controversial issue and review your opinions about it. See if you can reveal any internal or external standards, as well as core beliefs, that are at play in your overall response. Whenever you sense them contributing to a mental shutdown, don't stress or debate. Instead just open and allow, refocus and inquire, letting your resistance gradually release.

Releasing such resistance over time is what allows you to become more of yourself rather than less. Accepting the world as it is frees you to fight for the world you want. Such acceptance is the essence of Gandhi, of Mandela. It's what graces you with strength, endurance, and humility. It's also, as we'll explore further in the Seventh Invitation, our best hope for a peaceful planet.

NUMBING IDEAS

Thoughts that soothe can also
keep you shut down.

*R*esistance, as we've seen, is a refusal to accept what is. We resist our feelings by shutting down emotionally, and we resist reality by shutting down mentally. These two kinds of shutdowns often exacerbate one another. Unfelt emotions give rise to negative thoughts, and negative thoughts promote a lack of feeling. Accepting the first three Invitations puts an end to this debilitating cycle. But there is one type of resistance, subtler than the rest, which actually masquerades as acceptance.

Life's traumas and tragedies can bring forth intense emotion. Rage, grief, fear, and other overpowering feelings can be extremely difficult to open to fully. Instead, we may go numb. While common emotional shutdowns manifest as a pattern of physical tension, numbness diminishes all sensation. You can't tell what you're really feeling precisely because you can't feel. Numbness is a natural response to shocking events, but staying numb over a long period of time can keep both life and love at bay. Frequently, it's not just these events that keep us numb, but the ideas we have about why they're happening.

Do you tell yourself that everything happens for a reason? Do you believe that certain things are meant to be? Do you chalk up calamitous events to the will of God or the laws of karma? Sometimes such ideas are part of a fully conscious faith or viewpoint. Often, however, they keep us detached, witnessing life rather than engaging it. When this occurs, our emotions can pile up, even long after a stressful event, clamoring for attention and release. But since they're barricaded behind our resistant ideas, we don't even know they're present.

How can you tell whether a particular idea carries this numbing, resistant quality? Unfortunately, you can't look for a negative charge. In contrast to most resistant thoughts, numbing ideas don't carry one. Therefore, the next time you're in an emotionally difficult situation, be on the lookout, instead, for thoughts that seem new and unusual. If someone close to you died, for example, and for the first time ever you found yourself thinking, *We've all got to go sooner or later*, there's a good chance it would be a numbing idea. In addition, be watchful for sweeping philosophical thoughts, even the most seemingly benign, such as *I'm sure it's all for the best*. Finally, be wary of any thoughts at all that seem specifically designed to make you feel better.

If you do notice such an idea arising, turn your attention to your body. Can you actually feel every part of it? Are you open to the flow of sensation within it? Do you notice any emotion present? If the answer to all these questions is yes, then there's little numbness present and the idea probably isn't resistant. If the answer to any of them is no, then you're numb enough to address the issue.

Suppose you've just been diagnosed with a serious illness. After the shock wears off, you find yourself telling friends, "You know what, this is a wake-up call. It wouldn't have happened if my priorities were straight. In a way, I'm grateful." On the surface this sounds like acceptance. Viewing illness as an opportunity even seems like deep wisdom. But since you've never used the term "wake-up call" before, you heed this sign and turn your attention to your body. It's quite possible that you'd barely be able to feel your body at all. Or perhaps you'd sense some emotions present, but only faintly as if they were miles away. The discovery of such numbness would suggest that your thoughts, whether true or not, have been diverting you from disconcerting emotions. So instead of continuing to recite those thoughts, you'd keep your attention focused on your body.

The way to break through numbness is to pay very close attention to it. As you do, even the most protracted numbness will begin to dissipate. You may feel just a twitch here, or a tingle there, but such superficial sensations are enough to get the process going. By noting each sensation that breaks through, and keeping your attention on those that linger or strengthen, you restore your entire feeling mechanism. Almost always, if you continue to embrace what arises without any pressure or judgment, your numbness will eventually lift. In this case, once it's gone, you may find surges of fear, guilt, and despair. Once in touch with your true feelings, whatever they are, you might still refer to the illness as a wake-up call. Only now you'd be truly awake.

In the First Invitation we discussed the stories we sometimes tell ourselves to keep from feeling. Numbing ideas can be such stories in disguise. They're usually not about feelings at all, and only by paying attention do we uncover their repressive component. Recall some of the more difficult passages in your life. Perhaps you suffered great pain or loss. Perhaps you witnessed someone dear to you suffering likewise. Do you remember, during your darkest hours, falling back on any numbing ideas? Do you remember other people pressing their own numbing ideas upon you?

"It's good to keep busy." "Things could always be worse." Even when offered with great care, such sentiments can often encourage you to go numb. And what about the idea that "This, too, shall pass"? It will pass, whatever it is, unless reminding yourself of this over and over denies you access to all the feelings involved.

Love's challenge is to remain open at all times, even the worst. This means letting go of even the most comforting ideas if, and for as long as, their main effect is to keep you shut down. Meeting this challenge doesn't dissolve your most difficult emotions, but it creates the best possible environment for feeling them. Numbness, along with every other type of resistance, soon gives way to acceptance. Acceptance, now more than just a practice, begins to feel just like home. And when you're able to make a home of acceptance, love takes up residence, too.

ACCEPTING THE

THIRD INVITATION

To the best of my current and evolving ability, I resolve to:

- Review my personal standards
- Accept resistant thoughts one at a time
- Refocus unconstructive self-criticism
- Subject my core beliefs to inquiry
- Embrace people just as they are
- Release my resistance toward the world
- Free myself of numbing ideas

THE FOURTH INVITATION

Live Like You're Dying

When it's over I want to say: all my life

I was a bride married to amazement.

I was the bridegroom, taking the world into my arms.

—MARY OLIVER

In the Fourth Invitation love calls you to make

death your constant companion. The awareness of

death helps you heal old wounds, refine your

purpose, and lead a fearless, authentic life.

*W*hen will you die? After forty more years of a healthy and productive life? Or tomorrow, unexpectedly, right in the middle of updating your to-do list?

How will you die? Painlessly in your sleep without a trace of suffering? Or after a decade of agony, loneliness, and utter dependency?

Will you meet your death kicking and screaming, resisting its grip till your final gasp? Or will you surrender to death compliantly, gently, leaving the world in peace while welcoming whatever's next?

These questions are all rhetorical, of course, because the answers remain entirely unknowable. But whatever the eventual circumstances of your death, the reality remains—you *are* going to die. You're dying right now. Each breath you take brings you one breath closer to your last. In this way, even if you block it out completely, death is a vital part of life.

The topic of death is almost untouchable in contemporary society. We avoid talking about it if at all possible. We use euphemisms like "passed away" to refer to it. When our loved ones depart they're whisked out of sight by complete strangers. Sometimes we spend hundreds of dollars to artificially preserve the bodies so they look their best just prior to decomposition.

It's against the law to bury someone in the dirt, or in a blanket, so instead we spend hundreds more dollars to seal off the bodies in shiny caskets. These caskets are sold just like cars, with model lines and features to fit our exact level of budget and status.

All this adds up to one plain truth—there is nothing on earth we resist more than death. Resistance to death is what powers our endless fixations with youth, fame, and security. In each instance we seek solace in the illusion of a deathless life.

And then there's life after death. Many of us have specific ideas about what will happen after we die. Whether they center on heaven and hell or the wheel of reincarnation, these ideas can become numbing beliefs if held too tightly. They can create a seeming comfort with our eventual demise while at the same time shielding death's raw immediacy. The fact is that no one knows for sure what death will bring. To remain fully open in the face of death requires a rare and radical uncertainty.

Does such an approach seem stark, cold, and even unloving? It might, until you become familiar with the Fourth Invitation. This Invitation reveals, against all expectation, that death is life's greatest gift. The persistent proximity of death, when accepted completely, is what bestows life with radiant wonder.

People who love to skydive know firsthand the rush that risking death can bring. The heart races, the adrenalin flows, and through it all there's a sense of breaking through the daily monotony, of ripping away civilization's veneer. But when the event is over and the exhilaration fades, it's back to the same old routine.

The Fourth Invitation is about brushing against death not just in extreme situations, but at all times. It's about treating every moment like a free fall from thirty thousand feet. Minus the racing heart and the flowing adrenalin, it's a thrilling yet sustainable approach to life.

When you begin to live a life imbued with death, everything becomes more vibrant. Even life's most mundane and unpleasant aspects suddenly seem miraculous. It's akin to falling in love. Only now, instead of a person, the love object is life itself.

But life's renewed intensity is only the beginning. In its glow you begin searching every aspect of your existence for words unsaid, things undone, relationships unhealed, and time unwisely spent. With the finality of death ever present you reprioritize, focusing once and for all on what matters most.

Even with all these blessings, however, you may still find it difficult to accept the reality of death. It may trigger you profoundly, unconsciously. As a result you may overload your schedule with work, play, or just general busyness. Such distraction, in turn, makes welcoming death even more difficult, because it robs you of the time to do so.

Another difficulty in embracing death stems from the overwhelming nature of fear. Fear has two aspects: first, whatever you happen to be afraid of, and second, your fear of actually *feeling* fear. This second aspect is critical. Over the course of a lifetime the experience of fear can grow to seem unbearable, leaving you with a tendency to avoid new or difficult situations like an animal fleeing danger. As long as you're unwilling to open to fear, it's almost impossible to open to death.

That's why the first three Invitations are so important in preparing you for the fourth. Once you're ready to feel everything, fear of fear is welcome, too. Once you're ready to question everything and resist nothing, your limiting beliefs and judgments in relation to fear—such as *"I'm too fearful"* or *"Fear is cowardly"*—no longer hold much sway.

As you open to your fear of fear, gradually it begins to diminish. This encourages you to find the time and strength to keep going. Soon you're able to face each original fear itself. Perhaps it's fear of failure, loneliness, or humiliation. Whatever arises, you're willing to feel this as well. In the process you learn the language of fear. You learn to address it on its own terms. You learn to ask it the crucial question—*What's the worst that could happen?*

If I fail, what's the worst that could happen? If I'm lonely, or humiliated, what's the worst that could happen? And in the primal, irrational language of fear the answer is always the same—*I'll die*. No matter how trivial a fear may seem, no matter how specific or complex, at its core is the terror of annihilation. In other words, the force behind every single fear is a deeper, more fundamental fear of death. Even if this fear is more about the so-called death of the ego than the actual death of the physical body, it takes the same toll nonetheless.

In any other situation this would be grim news, yet here it's uplifting. Why? Because the one thing that can release you from the fear of death is the complete embrace of its inevitability. By accepting the Fourth Invitation, you overcome fear at its very core. With time, and an unwavering commitment, you render yourself virtually fearless.

Such fearlessness is what opens you beyond all openness. It's what connects you beyond all connection. It's what you need to love, and to let yourself be loved, with absolute abandon.

ILLUMINATING THE

FOURTH INVITATION

When you were born, you cried and the world rejoiced.

Live your life so that when you die,

the world cries and you rejoice.

—NATIVE AMERICAN PROVERB

BEFRIEND THE END

*Imagining your own death can mark
the beginning of freedom*

The Fourth Invitation, as we've seen, is about death. Not death as an abstract idea, but rather as a visceral reality. If you're like most people, you've spent years pushing this reality away. Therefore, actually feeling it can be quite a challenge.

Macabre as it may seem, one way to accomplish this is by imagining your eventual death in as much detail as possible. Start with your last breath, with the cessation of this form of consciousness. Picture your mind blanking, your heart ceasing, and your limbs slackening. There's no more you—the person you've been for all these years is dead, gone.

Now stand outside yourself, watch those attending you begin to mourn and console one another. Observe the ways they cope with the moment, from stoic stares to nervous humor. Picture them hugging, weeping uncontrollably, and sneaking in a few biting remarks between all the proper praise. If alive, these reactions would stir up a swirl of emotions within you. You'd feel compelled to engage, respond. In death, however, all you can do is witness.

Continue witnessing as your body is covered, transported to the funeral home, drained of blood and pumped full of embalming fluid, set inside a casket, left for a day or more, then wheeled to your gravesite and set deep into the ground. Remain attentive as prayers are read, and mounds of dirt are heaped upon you.

Years pass. Your skin and your insides wither. Soon you become nothing more than a skeleton, surrounded by thousands just like you.

Before bringing this exercise to a close, take it a step further. Spend one whole minute trying to wrap your mind around its own demise. Try to feel as if you were truly dead. This is impossible, of course, and your mind will quickly begin to rebel. But just accept the impossibility and continue, enacting the complete disappearance of all thought, sensation, and emotion.

If this visualization repulses you, or is troubling in any way, consider repeating it often. Feel free to change the details, or even the entire scenario. If you're still stuck, in need of a jolt, try spending an hour at a nearby cemetery. Wander among the corpses slowly, deliberately, staying mindful of all you think and feel.

For many, releasing resistance to death happens in layers, and takes considerable time. Throughout this process it helps to remember the purpose. Embracing your mortality makes every moment extraordinary. It quickens your entire being. It opens you more than almost anything else can. This new degree of openness removes many of your last and subtlest barriers to love. The more you bow to death, it turns out, the more you come to life.

DYING TO LIVE

When your awareness of death is complete,
life fills you with boundless gratitude

To render death even more vivid, imagine it's about to happen. Right now, no way around it. Without an opportunity to say goodbye or to get your affairs in order, all you can do is experience your existence for a few moments more.

Don't just read along. Give it your all. Make believe that you'll never have another chance to bite into a peach, swim in the ocean, or listen to a park full of joyous children. With the end so near, chances are such everyday occurrences suddenly become achingly precious. And what about things you normally disdain, like traffic jams, mosquito bites, and power failures. Somehow, at death's door, don't they become precious, too?

Surely you'll miss the wonders of nature—waterfalls, lightning, snow-capped peaks, and barren dunes. But won't you also miss less exalted landscapes, like run-down tenements, polluted rivers, and strip malls?

Isn't the same true of memories? In this final moment, reviewing all that's ever happened, don't you prize both the good *and* bad? And what about people? Clearly it will be hard to leave your loved ones. But consider those who hurt you, angered you, or just left you cold. Wouldn't you, if granted a reprieve, be thrilled to see them again as well?

You know that death has done its job when even the most difficult and miserable aspects of your life come to fill you with the deepest gratitude. Until then, there's still some resistance remaining.

Another way to make the possibility of death more immediate is to spend time with those who are actually dying. This may include people in your own circle, or hospice residents you volunteer to visit. Such a distinction doesn't really matter—when death is afoot, even complete strangers can grow suddenly close. Whatever benefit your presence provides the dying will be more than returned in kind. The experience allows you a rare opportunity to demystify death, and to taste the immensity of its sacred power.

A more popular approach to death contends that you shouldn't welcome it at all, that instead you should fight it with everything you've got. You're counseled, in the words of the poet Dylan Thomas, to "rage against the dying of the light." But how different is this sentiment, really? The only reason to struggle against death till the bitter end is that life itself is so dear. What matters isn't whether you shake your fist at death or wave it closer. What matters is your ongoing *awareness* of death, and that through this awareness you can live more fully.

The Fourth Invitation doesn't require surrendering your life even an instant before you must. If shaking your fist at death is part of a rallying cry for love, there's not a shred of resistance in it. But at times it can be a way of shutting down, of attempting to glorify that resistance. And when this happens, to some extent, aren't you a little dead already?

THE VOID

Stillness can connect you to your source.

How much free time do you have? What do you do with it? Would you consider doing nothing at all?

Free time is usually spent stepping away from the daily grind and replenishing oneself. This could include anything from fishing to mountain biking to carousing at the corner bar. During some of these activities the mind wanders. In others it locks into focus. Either way, at all times it's doing something.

Then there are those activities with a spiritual component, such as yoga, martial arts, and meditation. These disciplines have been proven to lower stress, quiet the mind, and bring about great healing. Even when bestowing such benefits, however, they often provide a cover for deeper turmoil. One of the few methods to uncover that turmoil, paradoxically, is ceasing activity altogether.

Doing nothing is harder than it seems. Try it for a few minutes and see. Attempt to make no movements, register no sensations, think no thoughts. Immediately your mind may rebel: *This is stupid, a waste of time. For God's sake give me a candle to stare at, a mantra to chant, or at least let me follow my breath.* Instead of a problem, this rebellion is valuable. It's exactly what's supposed to happen.

Try again. See how long it takes before doing nothing becomes staring at the back of your eyelids, falling asleep, or groaning in total frustration. Soon you come to understand that doing nothing is virtually impossible. This, too, is valuable, because now you can stop trying altogether. Doing nothing without effort or concern for failure ensures the least possible interference. The longer you're able to stay with it, the greater the reward.

The first reward for doing nothing is the opportunity to witness your customary response to real stillness. Your mind is likely so unaccustomed to this place that it flees from it like actual death. The thoughts, feelings, and drives that emerge usually have an edgy quality. They're about doing something else, anything else, as long as it gets you away from *this*. Once you learn to recognize this quality, you can look for it in daily life. Such avoidance may turn up in everything from excess work to compulsive exercise to seemingly harmless hobbies. Any activity, if unexplored, can become another subtle way to shut down.

The next reward for doing nothing is that it creates the time and space for your most buried emotions to surface. Your willingness to be still is what allows them the chance to move. By staying still, and feeling these emotions for as long as they last, you come to heal at a whole new level.

In addition, doing nothing leads you to realize how much of your life happens all on its own. Most thoughts do, as we discussed in The Power of Acceptance on page 82 but so, too, do perceptions, sensations, and emotions. For much of the time you're alive, life is actually living *you*. Stepping away from the illusion that you're in control of your entire existence enables you to relax, to let go more often and just be.

Finally, as you become able to approach the state of stillness with regularity, something remarkable happens. Whatever arises within the stillness does so more quietly and with less distraction. It recedes into the background. Into the foreground comes nothingness itself, the void, which you can then begin to experience directly. At first this experience may be scary, but if you stay with it the terrain soon becomes familiar. This is the formlessness out of which all being arises, the infinite space where all things join. It's where the "I Am" of your true identity resounds. In fact it isn't really empty, at least not in the conventional sense. As the birthplace of the entire cosmos, it positively overflows with love.

We touched upon the void in Who Am I? on page 49. Now we see that it's possible to return to it at will, and as a regular practice. Learning to tap into the void provides an ever-flowing wellspring of connection. This type of connection is akin to a peak experience, or to the complete absorption in activity known as "the zone." But these events are unpredictable and fleeting. The void, by contrast, is as steadfast as the beat of your heart.

REGRETS

Tending to unfinished business

ensures an open heart.

Once you begin to live like you're dying, it's clearer than ever before that each moment could truly be your last. This realization allows you to pursue deathbed reflections long before your time has come.

Looking backward at life, it becomes much easier to recognize all that you wish had been different. The variety of regrets is endless, but they fall into three main categories. The first category includes all the things you wish you hadn't done. The second category includes all the things you never got around to doing. The third and usually most painful category includes all your important relationships that remain strained or unresolved.

The first category has to do with choices. Whether about work, play, family, or love, in hindsight your choices seem mistaken or misguided. Perhaps you took a career track that proved unsuited to your passions and skills. Perhaps you never pursued a pastime that filled you with joy. Perhaps you married unwisely, even more than once, or took too stern an approach to your children.

Take a moment to write down all your most regrettable choices. Looking at the list may cause some serious pain. But if you open to the pain, rather than resist it, like all emotions it eventually passes. What's left is an opportunity to live the rest of your life differently, starting right now, with mortality as your constant reminder.

The second category is mostly about desire. It might contain regrets regarding books not written, sports not tried, trips not taken. It might also pertain to causes not championed, aid not offered, and friends not cherished.

Write down everything you'd like to do most in life but still haven't experienced. Keeping this list close at hand creates a great motivation to make these things happen before it's too late. It also allows you to revisit each desire from the standpoint of the previous three Invitations. That means finding and releasing any resistance that may have kept you from satisfying these desires till now. Such resistance may be emotional, like fear of failure or lack of self-worth. It may also be belief-based. You might have been thwarted by the kind of thoughts we discussed earlier, like "I shouldn't . . ." or "I'm not the kind of person who . . ."

Reviewing this list with the first three Invitations in mind also requires you to assess your motivations. Write down, beside each item, exactly why it's so important to you. But don't just stop at the obvious. See if you can determine your deepest drive. Suppose your list includes "*Own a lavish home.*" This might be motivated by a simple appreciation for aesthetics and comfort. But there also might be more to it.

You might write, *Other people will respect me.* If so, it's important to keep going, to ask yourself why you want to be respected. Often, as you can probably guess, it all comes back to love. If you were to realize that your deepest motivation for owning a lavish home is to feel loved, you could then inquire into the core beliefs implied. You may have a core belief, for instance, that love must be earned. Or you may have a core belief that love can only come to you from others. But are these beliefs true? The message of this entire book, to the contrary, is that love is available at all times to all who claim it. Remembering this would free you to keep pursuing your dream home or abandon it, knowing that love is yours either way.

The final category of regrets is about the heart as well, in particular about what happens when it's wounded. If a relationship between two people is strained or unresolved, they cannot fully open to one another. Often their greatest pain comes from the fact that such openness is precisely what they really want. No one ever went to the grave wishing to have loved less, yet sometimes feeling the intense hurt a relationship has caused seems even more difficult than remaining estranged. In some relationships you can ache to heal the rift, to clear the air once and for all, and yet somehow never begin.

Make a list of every person in your life that you regret not connecting with more. Since some troubled relationships just naturally fall away, or become irreparable, include only those people with whom you really do want to grow closer. Beside each name, write down why you haven't sought that connection till now.

You may be tempted to include reasons like lack of time or inconvenience. Even though these reasons may turn out to be completely accurate in your case, don't accept them without a little more probing. All busyness and difficulty aside, has there been even one brief opportunity to reach out? If so, and if you didn't seize it, might there be something else involved in your decision? Is it lingering hurt? Is it fear of more hurt? Remember, no one else is part of this evaluation but you. No one else is standing in judgment. With that in mind, allow yourself to uncover whatever answer feels truest for you.

Understanding the obstacles involved in healing relationships provides you with the opportunity to overcome them. Here, as before, the first three Invitations are invaluable. To begin you must feel everything. That includes all emotions about the relationship that have been shelved, even the oldest wounds. Next you must question everything about the relationship, especially any of your own opinions and assumptions that might prevent healing from taking place. Then you must conduct a search for all remaining resistance, including thoughts like *I just can't do it, I shouldn't have to,* or *It won't work anyway.* Meeting these thoughts with patient and gentle acceptance will, eventually, cause them to diminish and free you to move forward.

Delving into all your regrets, especially hurtful relationships, not only clears the way for love but is also love in action. If you're willing to give it a sustained effort, the Fourth Invitation yields its greatest treasure. In addition to reconnecting with yourself and those you love, you'll have time to relish that reconnection here on earth.

HARD TO HEAL

True forgiveness can't be

hurried or forced.

A re there wounds in your heart that just won't heal? Even after giving your all, are you still agonizingly stuck? Whenever this occurs, the missing piece is usually forgiveness. The idea of forgiveness is as compelling as it is popular. Until we learn to forgive, the conventional wisdom goes, we'll never be truly free.

The Fourth Invitation, however, takes a different tack. Forgiveness, just like love, is not something you can will into place. In fact, trying to forgive people can actually make forgiving them much harder. It can create significant mental resistance, giving rise to thoughts like *What's wrong with me? Why can't I just let go of this?* Such mental resistance may be powered by the internal standard "*I shouldn't hold on to grudges*" and the corresponding core belief that "*Grudges are wrong.*" Recognizing such standards and beliefs, and inquiring into their universality, most often will cause your resistance to release. It will allow you to accept yourself as you currently are, right or wrong aside, and foster the openness that forgiveness requires.

If you haven't forgiven someone, even after working through your mental resistance, it means that there's also an emotional shutdown occurring. To begin releasing the shutdown requires one critical question—*Is there something about this person that still angers or hurts me?* This question eventually brings its own answer, whether the buried feelings occurred yesterday or years ago.

Once these feelings are finally felt, forgiveness is the natural result. The Fourth Invitation is what paves the way. To live like you're dying means not just sitting back and waiting for these emotions to show up, but rather seeking them out, as if now is your very last chance, and opening to whatever you find. Doing otherwise is choosing to remain shut down. It presumes you have all the time in the world, and that holding on to your pain is worth the disconnection it can cause.

This point is so important it bears restating. A lack of forgiveness is generally a sign that you have been seriously wounded. In order to heal you must feel. Feeling the pain of your wound is the only thing that *can* heal it. This may seem totally unfair, as if in addition to the initial wounding now you're being punished again. Indeed, often it is unfair. Yet requiring fairness as a prerequisite to feeling only serves to keep you stuck. Drives for justice, retribution, or recompense may be necessary in certain cases, but they rarely bring about inner healing. Without a simultaneous commitment to plumb your own emotional depths, focusing on the offending party rarely serves you.

When people have been victimized by serious crimes, they often report that there is no closure. But closure isn't required to forgive, nor to love. To the contrary, opening is what's required. This is true whether the people involved are permanent fixtures in your life, or you'll never have anything to do with them again. It's true whether their actions were illegal, immoral, or just hurtful. Opening to your own pain, and your own vulnerability, is what brings about your own forgiveness. This forgiveness, first and foremost, is a gift that you give to yourself.

Along the way, while tending to your wounds, some of the emotions you'll feel may call for sharing. Others you might want to keep private. Either way, the job is wholly yours. While other people can ease your road to forgiveness, they're never responsible for it. Nor do they even need to be involved. Even if someone wounded you horribly and shows not a bit of remorse, it's still possible to let go of all your resistance, to feel all of the emotions that have been blocked, and to let forgiveness take root.

Be aware, though, that forgiveness obeys no timetable. In some cases, once you're willing to open to them, the feelings associated with a wound can dissipate quickly. In other cases they can take what seems like forever. It's tempting to downplay lingering feelings, even to deny them in an attempt to make peace, but such an attempt always backfires. The strain remains, and even if no one mentions it, everyone feels it.

When someone you haven't yet forgiven is a part of your life, and you'd like to treat that person as lovingly as possible, this simply entails telling the truth. "I'd really like to forgive you. I'm doing everything I am to let that happen. I'll stay as connected to you as possible until it does." Such a clear statement, as humble as it is heartfelt, is the best a real friend can offer.

MINE OR THEIRS

Authentic choices lead to

a loving life.

With the possibility of death ever present, you may find yourself planning each day's activities with a new sense of discrimination. *Is this what I really want to be doing? Are these activities vital or distracting? Am I fulfilling my highest potential?* Inevitably, things change. Not just in your daily schedule, but in your overall outlook. You begin to realize that until now many of your choices have been dictated largely by the expectations of family and community. It can be unsettling to see the extent to which you've relinquished your own life, yet this very realization is what enables you to begin gaining it back.

Let's begin right now. Divide your life into two categories, "mine" and "theirs." The mine category refers to life choices that are authentically your own, that you would continue to make even if they brought you no outside praise. The theirs category refers to any choices that are based mostly upon what others think, or what you assume they think. In this category you must also include reactive choices, meaning those that you've made primarily in opposition to any person or institution. In other words, when you've actively sought *dis*approval to make a point, those choices aren't all yours either.

Start with jobs, friends, hobbies, and fashion. If you're sure that your choices have nothing to do with sending cues to the outside world as a whole, or to any clique in particular, place them in the mine group. Suppose you're a doctor, and you simply love to practice medicine. What if the profession didn't pay well, carried no prestige, and brought only ungrateful patients? Would you still love it then? If so, it's definitely a mine. Suppose you love to play the electric guitar, even though you're not very good. That would proba-bly be a mine as well. But if the initial reason for playing was to drive your parents crazy, then it wouldn't qualify.

If you've pursued a course of conduct to appear smart, sexy, hip, or spiri-tual, place it in the theirs group. Have you ever hated a book but read it any-way, just because it was all the rage? Have you ever bought an outfit you thought was hideous because it was part of the current look? Have you ever bought an outfit you thought was beautiful but mostly to turn heads? Have you ever bought an outfit just because no one else was wearing it and you wanted to come across as independent? All of these choices are based mostly on how you believe others will perceive you, and as a result are clearly theirs.

Once you've catalogued at least at least five choices in each of the categories above, move on to consider the nature of your interactions in daily life. In what situations do you say what you honestly feel? In what situations do you shade the truth in order to manipulate how someone feels about you? This refers not only to winning approval, but also to avoid hurting the other person. No mat-ter how thoughtful or considerate your motivation, if a comment is not au-thentically yours, at least for now it's theirs. The same is true for visiting people you'd rather not see, or attending an event that you'd prefer to miss.

Since a list about daily interactions could go on forever, focus on the areas in which you find it hardest to live your truth. Do they involve authority fig-ures, competitors, or those who might withdraw their love? The choices you make with any of these people, or in your life as a whole, are bound to be multi-layered. Since we're all shaped to some degree by the prevailing culture, no choice can ever be exclusively mine. In addition, whenever you make a dif-ficult choice, some parts of you win out while others lose. The purpose of di-viding your choices into mine and theirs isn't to oversimplify. Instead, it's to find out how frequently, and how unconsciously, you give yourself away.

Once you become aware of this, and set out to live more genuinely, you're suddenly faced with a different problem. Without your previous mindset to lead you, decisions that were once automatic may now become difficult and confusing. Should you change your profession just because power and pres-tige might have motivated the choice originally? Should you start telling peo-ple exactly what you think even when it's most likely to hurt them? Should you boycott any social event that doesn't thrill you, regardless of the other purposes it may serve? If acting genuinely isn't the same as becoming saintly, uncaring, or inflexible, then what exactly is it?

This is where love comes in. When determining any course of action, simply ask yourself the following—*Which choice will open me more, will connect me to myself and the world around me in the most meaningful way?*

Let's look at some brief examples. If a coworker wants to know if you like her new hairstyle, and you don't, there might not be a need to share your whole truth. Instead of fostering openness and connection between you, bluntly stating your opinion might bring about the opposite. Therefore, you might turn the situation around and ask, "Do you like it?" After all, more than mine or theirs, this situation is really hers.

Now let's say your parents want you home for the holidays. You can't decide whether to go because the environment at family gatherings is usually caustic and hurtful. Attending out of guilt would seem to be theirs, and declining out of self-protection would seem to be mine. Yet obviously it's not that simple, since neither choice seems truly satisfying. In a case like this, you might need to share your whole truth. You might, with humility and respect, explain to your parents the exact nature of your trepidation. Of course you can't control how your parents will respond. They may get defensive, or attack you for even bringing up the subject. But such a response, though challenging, would still provide you with more information.

This information may lead you to decide that self-protection *is* actually mine, that it's required in this case even though not totally satisfying. But now your choice to stay away from the gathering would arise out of acceptance of the situation rather than resistance. You might feel sad, or lonely, or even guilty after all, but you'd be able to open to any of these feelings rather than acting them out. And if you did decide to go, for whatever reason, you could purposely keep your emotional distance. Such a boundary (we'll look more closely at boundaries in the Sixth Invitation) is the next best thing to total openness. It allows you to keep a clear channel to your own heart, and the love within it, even when those around you are unloving. It enables you to participate in any emotionally unsafe situation without being taken advantage of, and without becoming disconnected from yourself.

But what about when you must make a choice between two equally compelling options that both appear to be all mine? Imagine, for instance, that you have a limited amount of money to spend and can't decide whether to give it to charity or go on vacation. Clearly, there's no right answer. Both choices possess the likelihood to encourage openness and connection. In a case like this love isn't the deciding factor, but it motivates you to take a closer look. Would there be any resistance in either choice?

If you were leaning toward the charity option, such resistance in your decision making process may include thoughts like *Of course I should give the money away. Look how much privilege I already have. What kind of person can just loll around while others are in need?* Such intense justification might indicate that you'd really rather go on vacation. If so, what you'd be resisting is your own desire.

If you were leaning toward the vacation option, your resistance might include thoughts like *Why shouldn't I get a break every once in a while? It's not my fault people are in need. I shouldn't have to suffer just because they do.* In this case, your intense justification might indicate that you'd really rather donate the money. If so, again you'd be resisting your own desire.

Once you recognize this type of resistance in any train of thought, you're then able to accept it. You can also accept all your underlying desires. Regardless of whether you follow through on them, you'll no longer be at odds with yourself. Your final decision will come with less stress, and will feel as inclusive as it does authentic.

Learning to choose more authentically is an exhilarating process. It can drive you to make up for lost time, to make every decision count. Sometimes it's possible to experience this as pressure, not only to do the right thing but also to accomplish as much as you can. The Fourth Invitation isn't about pressure, however, but presence. It's not what you do that matters so much as how you do it. There's little love in lying on a tropical beach full of self-reproach, or in making a charitable donation while feeling personally deprived Once a choice is made, your mission is to own it, to stay open, and to embrace whatever unfolds.

PORTRAIT: THE SINS OF
THE FATHER

*J*orge's father was terminally ill with lung cancer. His two sisters and a brother were busy preparing for their dad's last days, but Jorge wasn't involved at all. Instead he threw himself headlong into his work as a junior college professor, making excuses about upcoming midterms.

Jorge received numerous emails about his father's worsening condition. None caused him to change his mind. He felt numb toward his father and judged himself for it, but the numbness had set in long ago. Telling his story at a workshop, Jorge showed almost no emotion.

From a very early age, all Jorge ever heard about from his father was money—how important it was, how you're nobody without it, and how each of his kids would take their place in the family textile company as soon as they graduated from college. Though Jorge had a head for business, he resented his father's obsession with it. The family, as Jorge saw it, always rated a distant second. So when the time came for him to join the business, Jorge flew the coop.

When compiling his list of regrets, Jorge realized that teaching was one of them. No matter how much satisfaction it brought him, he was constantly overworked and financially strapped. He also regretted the years of estrangement from his father, and how neither one of them could forgive the other for his choices. In fact Jorge had tried, many times. He'd read books on forgiveness and even prayed for it. But nothing worked, and since this only seemed to make him angrier, he eventually gave up and settled for a chilly distance.

While doing the "mine" or "theirs" exercise, Jorge realized something for the first time. He'd always thought his decision to become a teacher was all his own. But now it became clear that he'd made the choice partially to spite his father. Therefore, the decision really belonged in the theirs category. What's more, Jorge saw that he actually *blamed* his father for all the problems teaching presented. There was a part of him, illogical and immature though it might be, that felt his father had ruined his life.

This realization made Jorge incredibly guilty, which was a gift because it broke through his numbness. After opening to the guilt fully he felt a new desire to see his father, but also a great fear that it would go badly. His father hadn't changed, of course, only he had. Moving through the fear allowed Jorge to grasp that he had a task to accomplish regardless of how his father responded. If it merely led to more hurt, he would just move through that, too.

In a follow-up phone call after the workshop, Jorge described what had happened next. Instead of presenting a list of grievances to his father, or putting up a falsely loving front, he just described everything the workshop had revealed.

At first his father misunderstood, thought he was being blamed, and took it hard. He did a lot of yelling. Jorge focused on staying open, on connecting to the emotional flow in his body. This gave him the strength to communicate more clearly, to assure his father that nobody was truly at fault. In saying this Jorge saw that he really believed it. Forgiveness had finally happened to him, when he wasn't even striving for it. Hearing the shift in his tone, Jorge's father calmed down. Soon they were talking about everything that had been off-limits before. There wasn't any crying, nor were they suddenly joined at the heart. Still, they hadn't got along like this in years. Jorge was grateful to have begun living like he was dying before his father's death actually came.

BEYOND FEAR

As your terror of death begins to lessen,

most other fears diminish as well.

The overwhelming nature of fear, as we've discussed, is directly linked to death. To discuss this, however, is very different than experiencing it. Only by opening to fear in your own life, and watching very closely what happens, can you loosen its paralyzing grip.

The feeling of fear is the same no matter what instigates it. You can test this for yourself. Examine a strong fear the next time one comes up. It might be brought about by a serious storm, the sounds of a possible intruder, or the flashing lights of a police car in your rearview mirror. When it occurs, see if you can apply tools from the First Invitation to bring about some corresponding awareness. Use that awareness to recognize where the fear arises in your body. Does your gut clench? Does your breath stop? Does your heart pound?

This response, whatever the particular details, is as old as the first sentient creature. It's the survival instinct in action, a response to any perceived peril. The alarm sounded by fear is what activates your adrenalin, your fight-or-flight mechanism. In this state you become hyperalert, ready to do whatever it takes to avoid harm.

Once you've familiarized yourself with the feeling of intense fear, move on to track the more subtle variety. This might include fear of arriving late, of saying the wrong thing, of arousing someone's rage, or succumbing to your own. The next time a smaller fear occurs, whatever the cause, make the same examination as before. Notice exactly where it shows up in your body, and how your entire being responds. Chances are, you'll find that the response occurs in the exact same way.

Fear is fear. It varies only in duration and intensity. When you've seen this for yourself, the next step is to follow a small fear to its fullest expression. Suppose that you have an aversion to spiders, and that a harmless household variety is about to crawl on your face. In this instance, you stay put and allow the spider to come closer than you'd ever otherwise have allowed. The longer you remain still, and the closer the spider comes, the more likely your fear will reach unbearable proportions. You'll soon see that small fears aren't small at all, just easier to repress or avoid.

Now let's look at an interpersonal example. Imagine you're having an argument with your partner, who storms out before any possible resolution. Left thinking the relationship might be over, you're suddenly swamped by the familiar fear of abandonment. But this time, even though it feels strange and unnatural, you question the fear directly and turn its visceral response into words.

> *If the relationship is all over, what's the worst that could happen?*
> *I'll be left alone.*
> *If I'm left alone, what's the worst that could happen?*
> *There'll be no one to love me.*
> *If there's no one to love me, what's the worst that could happen?*
> *I'll be miserable.*
> *If I'm miserable, what's the worst that could happen?*
> *I won't be able to handle it.*
> *If I can't handle it, what's the worst that could happen?*
> *I'll fall apart, lose my job, and be homeless on the street.*
> *If I'm homeless, what's the worst that could happen?*
> *I'll be murdered, or starve, or freeze to death.*

There it is. Ultimately, no matter how long it takes, death makes an appearance. Logically, you're well aware that the end of a relationship is not life threatening. But as you've surmised by now, fear has nothing to do with logic.

For the purposes of the Fourth Invitation, fear is to be both respected and welcomed. Beyond that, it's even to be encouraged. When you open to a smaller fear completely, which then reveals its essence as the fear of death, what follows is a watershed moment. In a wordless exchange you make it clear—*Death is around the corner, always. I don't run from it. I bow to it. It makes everything immediate, sacred.*

In the wake of such unqualified acceptance, almost all fears begin to lose their force. Eventually there's no more fight, no more flight, just a rare and empowering peace.

ACCEPTING THE

FOURTH INVITATION

To the best of my current and evolving ability, I resolve to:

- Confront the reality of my death
- Savor each moment as my last
- Cultivate absolute stillness
- Tend to my unfinished business
- Be patient in my attempts to forgive
- Make the most loving choices
- Follow my fears to freedom

THE FIFTH INVITATION

Live Like You're Dreaming

In dreams and in love

there are no impossibilities.

—JANOS ARANY

In the Fifth Invitation, love calls you to awaken to

the power of your unconscious. This power leads

you to new depths of personal insight, and infuses

your life with possibility and wonder.

*I*n a dream, there are no rules. Nothing can be taken for granted. One minute you're blown to bits in a bloody wartime trench, the next you're negotiating with gophers over their share of your summer garden, and then suddenly you're in the middle of a volcano, ecstatic, scooping up the popcorn it erupts.

A dream mystifies. A dream astounds. A dream, above all, keeps you forever on your toes.

What would your life look like if you lived it as a dream? How would it be different? How would *you* be different?

When you get out of bed each morning, for the most part the world seems the same. The toilet can't speak Greek, the coffee won't foretell your future, and the paper doesn't announce its headlines with a rousing song and dance. The consistency of daily events creates a sense of predictability, of routine.

But let's rewind. When you get out of bed each morning, what's your state of mind? Are you excited and raring to go, or do you have to pry yourself away from the covers?

As you step into your slippers, what sounds are present? Birds, buses, shrieking kids, or whirring fans? Do these noises grate or soothe, coax you forward or set you back?

While you shower, are your movements easy or stiff? Have old pains returned or new ones arrived? Or, pleasantly, is your entire body supple and free?

Finally, once you've sat down to scan the news, what stories pull at your gut, or hurt too much to take in, or arouse a wry smile, or remind you that you're late for work?

Beyond the basic activities they share, no day is like any other. For that matter, no moment is like any other. The more attention you pay to the moments that make up your routine, the more they reveal themselves in unique and exquisite detail. When you bring the wide-eyed, ever-curious approach of your dream-self into everyday waking existence, suddenly the difference between the two realms seems to diminish. Both are rich in subtlety, resonant with depth, and full of endless surprise.

When life has gone a certain way for long stretches of time, we may begin to assume that it will always be that way. While applicable to daily events, this is especially true for long-standing patterns related to success and failure, and love and loss. It's so easy to think, *I've never been successful till now, so tomorrow won't be any different.* Or, *Since I've never found lasting love, there's no reason to assume that will change.* These beliefs frequently exist at the deepest level, beneath all evidence to the contrary.

Such beliefs may seem like the result of depression or low self-esteem, but actually the opposite is true. To shrink one's sense of potential based solely on past experience—what could possibly be more arrogant? It's a way of playing God, of damning the entire future before it ever has a chance to arrive. And, tragically, it works. In a landscape of unyielding pessimism, there's no room for life's bounty. Like love, it can't go where it's not welcome.

To live life as a dream requires a radically different approach. It means surrendering arrogance for humility, certainty for possibility, and a closed mind for an open heart. In the process of this transformation, life becomes a waking dream. It's no less real, or vital, yet suddenly everything's more striking, more fluid. Fewer things trip you up or shut you down. You become present to your experience in a fuller way than ever before. And that presence is the gateway to greater love. You feel it inside, bestow it upon others, and evoke it in them all at once.

As with any dream, the dream of your life is open to interpretation. This means things aren't just what they seem. Instead, they're much more. No detail is insignificant; no point of view is complete. The more you're willing to dig, the more treasure you're bound to unearth.

All the people you encounter, when approached in this way, become not just individuals but characters. Each one has something specific to represent, and fits uniquely into your overall dream. A needy friend might tap into a life-long motif about giving, receiving, and finding the proper balance between them. A conniving coworker might embody the theme of conflict, helping shed light on how you seek it, avoid it, or perhaps unknowingly exaggerate it. Even the stunning waitress, the sickly beggar, and the vulgar kid on the plane—though crossing your path ever so briefly—still have a role to play. Your response to each incidental character can speak volumes, as long as you're willing to listen.

The same is true of events. When you crash your car, get a call from an old lover, or misplace your watch three days in a row, it's never entirely random. There's always a connection to draw, a significance to discover. Opening to this significance doesn't require you to become overly analytical or narcissistic. Nor does it imply a filtering of life through any particular lens, be it religion, psychology, philosophy, astrology, or any other. All that's needed, ever, is a little bit of time and imagination.

Nowhere does life gain more as a dream than in the realm of memory. The life stories we construct for ourselves usually include a single plot, with a small list of key people, places, and turning points. These stories often center on what has marred us, and what we've attempted to overcome in our quest for fulfillment. They're frequently what we bring to therapy or other healing pursuits, attempting to free ourselves from the past once and for all.

But in dreams, nothing is more important than anything else. When seeking the most illuminating interpretation, it's important to consider the entire dream. If you focus only on certain events, or on just one narrative thread, you often miss the details ripest for discovery. A dream may seem as though it's solely about a road trip and all the characters along the way, until you realize that the road itself is made of wedding gowns, and the gas in your tank is actually expensive champagne.

Your past, in the same way, is much richer than any single biography. This is due to both the unconscious and conscious aspects of memory formation. On the unconscious side, your brain's data bank logs just a portion of your full life experience. And of that portion, a vastly smaller one becomes available for recall. This means that you're unable to remember the majority of your own life. You simply don't know what happened during those forgotten stretches, and whether it was significant or not.

On the conscious side, each time you do recall a memory, that memory strengthens. And when you continually focus on your prevailing biography, the memories associated with it strengthen out of proportion to all the rest. Even important memories that *are* available for recall may fade or disappear entirely without periodic access. This is especially likely if those memories fall outside the scope of, or contradict, the "official" life story you tell yourself.

By viewing your memory as a dream, you avoid getting trapped in any one story's limitations. You recognize that what brought you to this moment, and made you who you are, is more than you can ever know. No one is *just* the product of a broken home, or the survivor of a terrible accident, or the one who was so painfully shy. Your own early setbacks and obstacles, whatever they were, can be offset, lightened, and even transcended by seeking out parallel tales. No matter how much of your past is no longer available, there are always additional memories to retrieve.

You may, for example, have suffered from serious emotional neglect as a child. You may have spent years of counseling and thousands of dollars to unravel the effects. From the dream perspective you don't refute or minimize a memory of neglect, but rather you add to it. You begin to search for recollections, or even just possibilities, of childhood experiences that were uplifting and beneficial. You stretch your perspective to include other important themes beyond those of home and family. In time, this process bears abundant fruit. By multiplying the meaning of your past, you inevitably expand your present.

Similar expansions also occur in you, the dreamer, as you accept the Fifth Invitation. Recognizing the way your identity shifts from dream to dream allows you to employ the same flexibility in daily life. When it's necessary to be brash and outrageous, you rise to the occasion. When the moment calls for subtlety and tenderness, you dial yourself down. At no time do you lock into any single type of behavior. At no time does any one trait block out all the others.

Once you allow yourself to be everything you are, it seems that you're many people at once. At work you're a lion, and at home you're a lamb. In social settings you're reserved, while one-on-one you're gregarious. With others you're generous, yet with yourself you're stingy. Instead of bemoaning this, or attempting to fix it, as a dreamer you embrace it totally. You recognize that your greatest strength comes not from uniformity, but diversity.

In particular, you pay great heed to your weaknesses, your faults, everything about yourself that you'd rather wish away. Understanding how dreams can reveal pieces of yourself that are otherwise denied, you now look for similar revelations in your waking world. Instead of shrinking from these shadows, you welcome them. Becoming intimate with your shadows, you realize, is the way to become intimate with yourself.

As all this happens—finding new significance in people and events, expanding your life story and yourself, reconnecting with your shadows—you begin to feel held, nurtured, and even loved just for the very fact of your existence. You can't quite tell, and it doesn't really matter, whether the source of this love is without or within. It feels as if who you are is nearly indistinguishable from everything you perceive and experience. Without losing your personal sense of identity, you find yourself equally identified with this larger whole, and especially with the love that knits it all together. The more you love, the bigger you grow. You become dedicated to such continued unfoldment, which adds a stirring sense of purpose to your dream.

In addition, the more skilled a dreamer you become, the more control over your dream you possess. This control can extend all the way to lucid dreaming, or the ability to change the course of a dream with the power of your own intention. Lucid dreaming works as well in daytime as it does at night. It's neither magical nor mysterious. It's merely a way of focusing your energy on any patterns, perceptions, or personas that have grown stagnant and limiting. You replace these dead ends with the dream of a different future. You encourage, entice, and love that future to life.

Regardless of when the future occurs, or whether it ever transpires at all, you hold the story of your life more gently. You learn, whatever the eventual outcome, not to take it too seriously. In the end it's all just a dream. It can change at any moment. You can change at any moment. And with such a liberating perspective, you often will.

ILLUMINATING THE

FIFTH INVITATION

There are only two ways to live your life.

One is as though nothing is a miracle.

The other is as if everything is.

—ALBERT EINSTEIN

REFRAME THE MUNDANE

There's endless magic and mystery

even where you least expect it.

Daily life is bound to be filled with periods of drudgery and boredom . . . or is it? To live like you're dreaming means revisiting all the aspects of your life that have grown routine. By investing them with sensuality and imagination, the "same old" can become surprisingly fresh.

Take housework. Dusting is merely a chore, and the stray spiderweb just out of reach is nothing but a nuisance. But then, rather than exploring your possible fear of spiders as in the Fourth Invitation, now you may wonder what it would be like to be one. Would you enjoy spending most of your time suspended in midair, gliding from place to place on a self-made trapeze? How about those eight legs—would they ever trip over one another? Would you ever doze off during the long waits for dinner? And what's the deal with those giants, hundreds of times your size, that run screeching whenever they cross your path?

Even if there's no spiderweb in sight, how do you usually tackle a room? Do you work ceiling down, or floor up? What about, for once, allowing your dusting to become a dance? Let the rag sweep across the coffee table in dramatic figure eights. Feel the smooth, cold window frame with the tip of every finger. Buff the stereo cabinet with your behind. When you start to feel silly and self-conscious, don't push the feelings away. Instead give them expression. What song would they sing? How would they move to it? If you end up on the floor, making a complete fool of yourself, that's the perfect time to dust under the couch.

There's nothing especially virtuous about cleaning. You may hire someone to do it and never look back. But if you can't afford such a luxury, and are stuck with housework on a regular basis, then it's as engaging as you choose to make it.

That's equally true about other routines, such as the morning and evening commute. You can stress out and resist till it's over, or turn the entire journey into a dream. Next time you hit the road, for example, consider the view through your windshield. Is the sky cloudy or clear, blue or gray? What else can you think of that's the exact same color?

Now roll down the window, if you're not surrounded by exhaust, and take a deep breath. Does the air have a scent? Is it moist or dry, hot or cool? When can you remember breathing air just like it? Let your sense memory make the connection. Then, while still keeping your eyes on the road, transport yourself back to that time. What people stand out most strongly? What would you want to tell them, right now, if they suddenly appeared at your side? What would they see out the window that you don't? How would they perceive it differently?

You're as alive as you are curious, no more or less. Beyond cleaning and driving, take a moment to reflect on any of your other activities that may have grown stale. Could you possibly dream them back to life? Could you open yourself to them with as much enthusiasm as you bring to your favorite activities, thereby opening to love as well? If so, how soon are you willing to begin?

From time to time, no doubt, you'll forget. Best intentions aside, your eyes will still glaze over. Such an occurrence isn't a failure—it's a challenge. Right then, whether in your own mind or the immediate surroundings, look for whatever's bound to wake you up.

REPEAT PERFORMANCE

Painful life patterns are appeals

from your unconscious.

While it's a mistake to assume that things will always be the way they've been, it's also true that they sometimes follow certain patterns. Ignoring the existence of familiar cycles keeps you shut down, and is therefore a barrier to love.

Before reading on, make a quick and candid assessment of any detrimental patterns in your life. Do you keep racking up debt in spite of all your best efforts? Do you always seem to attract demanding bosses? Do you continually lose friends over the same issue?

When things happen in your life again and again, especially if you strive mightily to change them, the Fifth Invitation becomes an invaluable tool. Instead of beating yourself up or admitting defeat, you can view these patterns as a recurring dream.

A recurring dream is usually a call for attention from your unconscious. Until you get the message the dream will likely continue. To get the message you don't take the dream at face value but instead seek out its deeper meaning. The motif of a marauding bear probably isn't about your fear of wild animals. Nor would the theme of falling tend to represent your fear of heights.

Clearly, the language of the unconscious is suggestive, symbolic. What's not so clear is how it's also spoken in waking life. Just as a recurring dream compels you to stop, to investigate, so, too, does a troubling pattern of events. The gift of a pattern, once you're willing to explore it, is that it calls you to something beyond your awareness. And what your exploration reveals, almost always, is a long-neglected emotional shutdown.

Unlike nighttime dreams, waking ones require no interpretation. All you need to do is apply the First Invitation and feel what has been previously blocked. To do this means letting the emotions of a pattern arise completely. It means following them gently to their source.

To begin, let's look at a relatively simple example. Say you're constantly late for work, no matter how early you set the alarm. It's a new habit but one you can't seem to break. And with each late arrival comes a corresponding surge of guilt. Your unconscious keeps creating the opportunity for you to feel guilty, but why? The next time you're late, instead of resisting the guilt, you lean into it. And suddenly an image flashes of an office associate to whom you were recently rude. It's clear, in that same moment, that you've felt guilty about the rudeness ever since but have been pushing the feeling away. As soon as you're ready to welcome it, all of it, there's a good chance you'll start arriving on time.

Can you know for certain that the two incidents are directly connected? No. Is it possible that your lateness will continue? Of course. But by viewing your pattern as a recurring dream, you've made an important emotional discovery regardless. And remember, every reclaimed emotion causes you to open just a bit more. Such an opening enables you greater access to love, to both the feeling and sharing of it. Even though it may not seem so at first, the ultimate reason for unraveling a pattern is to loosen its hold on your heart.

Now let's examine a much deeper pattern. Suppose you attract the same type of unloving partner again and again. The faces, names, and personalities are different each time, but your sense of loneliness hardly changes. Perhaps you've already explored the situation in workshops, or therapy, and discovered that it all stems from serious childhood wounding. Yet in spite of this information, and even though you "reprogram" yourself to make different choices, somehow you seem stuck at square one. You're stuck there, in this case, because recognition and understanding are not enough. Whenever a backlog of emotions is so big, there's a corresponding amount of resistance to release.

While there are many techniques available to aid in this process, the only essential ingredients are time and willingness. You may want to journal in stream of consciousness about how the hurt began, including every detail that arises and stopping frequently to feel the effects. You may want to speak the story out loud to a trusted friend, forgetting about the clarity of your words and focusing on the emotions they elicit.

Many people need to move through so much fear, shame, and judgment about early wounding that it can take a lot of patience to reach the original feelings. They also worry about getting stuck in blame, or dwelling too much in the past. That's why it's important to remember that unfelt emotions live in the present, that they affect the present, and that finally feeling them helps diminish blame rather than increase it.

Feeling the full pain of childhood wounds may take months or even years. Echoes of it may linger forever. At the same time, however, there *is* a definite healing threshold, a point at which you become fundamentally free. How do you know you've reached that point? Not because the pattern doesn't persist. It may always persist to some degree. What changes more than anything is your response to it. You recognize it earlier, get drawn in less often, and find yourself able to make different choices. These changes ripen in you, season over time, until eventually the pattern seems less like doom and more like just an aspect of your makeup. You may even find yourself regarding the pattern with tenderness and gratitude for the opportunity to grow.

THE BIG PICTURE

To love life fully can require broadening

your story of the past.

Nothing is more like a dream than memory. They both exist only in the mind's eye. They both evoke strong feelings, fade in and out of clarity, and lead us to frequent reflection. Yet for the most part we approach them from opposite angles. Dreams we interpret, gaining more perspective the deeper we delve. Memory, on the other hand, we tend to approach like a collection of facts. We look upon the past as a static reality, existing apart from our own perceptions.

To accept the Fifth Invitation is to comprehend that memories *are* dreams, neither true nor verifiable in an objective sense. While some details of your past can certainly be substantiated, memories of that past are comprised primarily of subjective impressions and sensations. If this doesn't immediately ring true, pick a few key early memories and share them with the members of your family. Ask to hear their versions of the same events. Almost always there's significant variation.

Acknowledging such variation means opening your memories to new scrutiny. It means realizing that any particular set of memories may not be fully reliable, complete, or understandable without additional context. When stories from your past have kept you shut down and disconnected from others, revisiting them with an expanded perspective can help free you from their grip. It can open you when other methods fail, providing valuable support in your pursuit of love.

Let's return to the earlier example of parental neglect. Because it's extreme, this topic can help demonstrate the great benefit of memory expansion. Once you've read the following demonstration through, pause for awhile and ponder your own most difficult memories. Then expand them, whether extreme or not, using the three steps outlined below.

Serious neglect at the hands of a parent is sure to leave a host of painful memories. Excavating and working through these memories in some kind of counseling is almost always valuable. But perhaps the worst legacy of such neglect is the way it can blot out all the normal, and even extraordinary experiences from the very same childhood.

To fully retrieve the rest of such a childhood, you'd begin by cataloguing all the experiences that brought you respite, relief, and even pleasure. These can be as simple as a favorite flight of fancy, a comic book, or a neighborhood park. They can consist of special friendships and engrossing hobbies. It's important to note that they can also include tears, rage, or even adolescent rebellion if it kept you from numbing completely. The point is that all such memories carry their own independent vitality. By retrieving them, and revisiting them often, you contribute to your own liberation.

The second step in memory expansion involves mining your past for additional life stories. Neglect, no matter how serious, is always just one story among many. Other stories would abound in your connections with siblings, relatives, friends, and the world around you. The stories you'd be looking for aren't merely incidents or relationships. They're much broader, containing rich themes and defining elements in the shaping of your sense of self.

Have you struggled, for instance, with poverty or privilege? The theme of money, almost always, is potent enough to create a lifelong saga. Have you consistently compared yourself to a central person in your life, or to an ideal? Comparison is also the source of many life stories. So too are themes of passion, including the search for it and the lack of it, whether in work, love, or life in general.

There are only a certain number of major themes, but the stories they spawn are as varied as the people who live them. The goal of seeking out your own stories is to realize that for as long as you can remember, you've always been the hero of *many* tales. To lock into any one of them, and to limit your self-perception to its confines, is like dreaming in black and white.

The third step in memory expansion is the most challenging, and should only be undertaken with lots of care, support, and time. It requires you to view your memory through the eyes of its "villain." This means not just trying to understand your neglectful parent, but instead actually imagining yourself *as* that parent.

If you're really ready, not pushing beyond your current capacity, then trading places in this way can bring about great discovery. At first it might strike you that your role as parent included far more than neglect. If your neglect was primarily emotional, then perhaps to some extent you were a provider, a guardian. Perhaps you drove your child to school, to doctor appointments, and tended to the other basics of everyday care. Conversely, if everyday care was the main area of your neglect, then perhaps you were at least somewhat emotionally present. Perhaps you often expressed feelings of affection, of connection, even if unable to follow through with your actions.

And then, of course, there is the possibility that you were deficient in both aspects of parenting. Rather than just neglectful, maybe you were totally absent. But even if that's the case, what gave rise to such absence? Chances are it stemmed from some kind of brokenness, or an inability to connect with your own heart. And what did that absence actually feel like to you? Most likely, beneath any denial or defensiveness, it filled you with sadness, regret, and guilt.

None of this, keep in mind, is about excusing what's inexcusable. But it can lead to profound healing. As soon as there is no villain, then there's also no longer a victim. In place of these one-dimensional stereotypes are actual human beings—flawed, conflicted, and maddeningly complex.

Just as in a dream, the personas we all present in waking life are infinitely varied and prone to shift in a flash. When you're able to see the people of your past in this light, your judgments about them soften. You soften. And your heart, leaping at the opportunity, gathers in those who once were banished.

ROLE PLAY

Everyone you meet is an outward

expression of yourself.

*A*ccording to a common method of dream interpretation, all the characters in your dreams represent different aspects of you. The way to glean the full meaning of any dream, from this perspective, is to relive it through the eyes of each character. You experienced a version of this in the previous Illumination, and saw how it can transform your view of another person. Inhabiting dream characters from the inside out, additionally, can transform the way you view yourself.

Suppose you have a dream about being stalked down a dark alley by a hulking criminal. Revisiting the dream from the viewpoint of the protagonist, the "I" of the dream, might lead to sensations of panic and terror. Investigating these sensations further might uncover some previously unconscious fears about what's currently happening in your life.

Next you'd imagine yourself back into the same scene, only this time as the stalker. While at first you might feel predatory and vengeful, the longer you stay in character, the greater likelihood of additional revelation. For example, you might find yourself frustrated, even guilty for having to pursue your victim this way. Perhaps you've been trying to get noticed for months, or even years, only to be rebuffed at every turn. It's possible that from the beginning you've only had a simple message to deliver. Maybe it's that you're not as strong as you look, that you're tired of always pretending to be so powerful, and that all you really want is to let down your guard.

Playing the role of the stalker, in this case, would acquaint you with an aspect of yourself that seems long suppressed. You'd have the opportunity to ex-plore it, evaluate it. *Are* you as strong as you seem? Do you sometimes exag-gerate your power? Would it be a relief to let down your guard?

Applying this type of dream expansion in your waking life requires noth-ing less than a revolution in perspective. It means that every person you come across, from your boss to your minister to your latest flirtation, is actually a piece of you. You don't just accept this as a truism, like "God has many faces." Instead, you actually relate to the people in your world as outward expressions of your own being.

Say you have an arrogant uncle who always belittles you. Normally you choose to avoid him or fight back. Now, however, you seek to step inside him, to see what he sees and feel what he feels. Inevitably, this provides great insight into his behavior. Maybe your successes remind him of his own fail-ures. Maybe his customary haughtiness conceals a deep self-hatred. Recog-nizing the all-too-human motivation behind his arrogant and derisive façade might allow you to stop resisting those qualities so much. And once you've accepted them a little more in him, you could search for similar qualities in yourself.

You might argue that to approach your uncle in this way lets him off the hook, and that he's still free to be the same old jerk while you're doing all the inner work and personal growth. But seen from an openhearted point of view, he might somehow be contributing perfectly, in all his unpleasantness, to the grand scheme of things. It's not for you or anyone else to know, and certainly not to judge. In addition, if you're inspired to confront your uncle in the hopes of changing his behavior, what could possibly improve your chances more than the discovery of so much common ground?

You might also argue that you're not arrogant or derisive in the least, and that, on the contrary, you're actually quite humble and supportive. But a fun-damental tenet of the Fifth Invitation is that each one us has the capacity for all types of behavior. We are both the individual dreamer and the whole dream. We identify with different parts of ourselves to varying degrees, yet still they're forever present.

"Playing" your uncle would allow you to *feel* what it's like to be arrogant and derisive. It would enable you to recall times when you felt the same way, even if to a lesser degree. Have you ever acted the least bit superior to someone else? Have you ever slightly exaggerated your own achievements? If you can't honestly remember such times, ask those who know you best for a little assistance. Once you've found some occurrences, you've also found a hidden streak of arrogance.

Have you ever found fault in someone when it wasn't necessary or helpful? Have you ever made fun of people when it was likely to hurt their feelings? If you can't honestly remember such incidents, check in once again with those who know you best. Once you've found some, you've also found a hidden streak of derision.

Sometimes, after discovering or revisiting distasteful parts of yourself, it's easy to accept them. Other times it's much more difficult. In these cases, refocusing can be of great assistance. Your initial reaction, for example, might be something like, *I can't believe I'm just like my uncle! It's disgusting! And all this time I was feeling holier than thou.* After refocusing, you may come to the following assessment: *At times I'm arrogant and derisive. It's uncomfortable to recognize. But it's also something I'm free to work on.*

Inquiry, too, can help you accept distasteful qualities. When exploring the issue of arrogance, you might uncover a personal standard such as *I should always be modest.* Underlying that standard might be the core belief that *Modesty is good.* But is it always good? Aren't there times when a little self-congratulation, or even exaggeration, could help you through a daunting task? And even if you don't believe that's true, aren't we all allowed to have a few flaws?

Once you're comfortable seeing others as an expression of yourself, emphasize the process for a week or so. Briefly take on the personas of all the main characters who cross your path. Try to see and feel the world as they do. Stay away from any possible negative perceptions of you, however, as they can lead to unnecessary shutdowns. And don't worry about becoming presumptuous in your appraisals—for right now these are just characters in *your* dream. If you can't really draw a bead on some of them, ask questions. Invite them to reveal themselves to you. When people sense your genuine interest, they almost always open up.

At the end of this exploration, review your whole list of characters. Do you seem to have more in common with them than before? Have they helped uncover anything new about you?

Each time you repeat this type of role play, it can bring you a little closer to the world, to yourself, and to love. The way of love is to embrace all human qualities, and everybody who possesses them, with equanimity and compassion. This applies even to those traits that seem unloving, unlovable, or both. Love doesn't condemn, deny, or separate. It only connects. The ability to see ourselves in others, and they in us, is perhaps the world's greatest healing force.

MULTIPLICITY

The more you welcome all your separate selves,

the more connected you grow as a whole.

*I*n the Second Invitation, Question Everything, we looked at many possible limitations in the way you see yourself. They included overidentification with family and social roles, outdated beliefs, and one-sided self-judgments. Now let's return to the issue of self-perception. By viewing yourself through the lens of the Fifth Invitation, you can dream a fuller, more unified, and more loving sense of identity.

Already we've seen how playing the different characters in your life reveals lesser-known aspects of yourself. But once you know they're present, what are you supposed to do about it? To begin, for a few days, pay specific attention to all the moments when you find yourself at odds, when the way you want to feel and act is quite different from how you actually let yourself behave.

Do you sometimes want to plop your head down and take a nap in the middle of a business meeting, only to instead hoist yourself ramrod straight? Do you ever have random sexual thoughts about the most inappropriate people, only to shut them down with disapproval before they really get going? Often, when your moods, responses, and drives don't match who you think you are or should be, an inner battle ensues. But a short-lived victory can turn into an embarrassing loss. Suppose your thoughts are often catty, for example, filled with ridicule for others that you won't even let yourself open to silently. Sooner or later, perhaps at the worst possible time, one of those comments is bound to pop out.

Squelching any part of yourself isn't dreamlike at all. In fact, it's another type of resistance. So once you've taken a closer look at these moments of self-opposition, it's time to start living them as a dream. Now, nothing is out of bounds. Every stray thought and random impulse is welcomed with wonder, even if you don't express it or act it out. You no longer pretend that your internal life obeys any rules whatsoever. Instead you surrender to the anarchy, revel in it, and as a result spring fully to life.

Rather than a single identity, in truth you're a multiple personality. If there's a well-mannered you, there's also an indecent you. If there's an open-minded you, there's also a know-it-all you. What makes this healthy, as opposed to pathological, is that once you're aware of all your selves, it's possible to roam freely among them. The less you attempt to restrict or banish them, the more they come together as a whole.

Though this perspective may seem abstract, it has enormous practical benefit. If you generally see yourself as a busy, outgoing person, you will no longer think that something's wrong when you're struck by periods of melancholy and isolation. If you generally see yourself as a peaceful, nonviolent person, you will no longer feel mortified when given to fantasies of murderous rage.

In the dream of your life you shape-shift constantly, opening to any self that makes an appearance. This opening creates more love for yourself, which in turn creates more love for others.

Over time you may notice that certain selves recede, and that others rise to take their place. Since you're not clinging to any fixed set of characteristics, this state of flux feels less like crisis and more like adventure.

Why not get the adventure started right now? Draw a big circle and divide it in half. In the top half list all the selves with whom you're most comfortable and familiar. Give them names, like the Hard Worker, the Pleaser, the Spendthrift, and so forth. There may be just a handful or a whole dozen. On the bottom half of the circle list all the selves that you're aware of but judge harshly or don't usually indulge. Mirroring the selves above, this list might include the Goof Off, the Narcissist, and the Tightwad. Here, too, the total amount of selves may be large or small. Not all the ones you place in either half of the circle need be opposites, nor clearly positive or negative. You're likely to assess many selves, both familiar and less known, as somewhere in the middle. Such selves might include the Flirt, the Eccentric and the Joker.

When you've completed this personal pie chart, keep it with you for a few days and see how representative it really is. Would it be more accurate if the top half became nine-tenths of the circle? Do you allow yourself enough time to roam toward the bottom? At the end of each day, shade in any self in the circle that got some real quality time without interruption from the others. Make it your goal that by the end of the third day the entire circle is shaded. Then put a note in your calendar to redraw the circle in another six months, adding, removing, and shifting any selves as necessary.

As you create greater equality among your wide range of selves, parallel shifts often occur in your life. You make different kinds of friends, some who might share little in common with one another. You seek out a broader scope of activities, even if they don't seem to jell. A punk rocker who does needlepoint is truly a free spirit. So is a jock who loves poetry, a bungee-jumping priest, or a meditating CEO.

With each dream you're someone new. So too with each day, each hour, and sometimes even each moment. Make a habit of asking yourself, *Who am I right now? What selves am I avoiding or ignoring? Which ones are desperate to get a word in edgeuise, to take a rest, or, just for a little while, to grab hold of the reins and ride?*

NIGHT VISION

*Reclaiming the darkest parts of yourself is
the key to unconditional love.*

*A*mong your many selves, there will always be those you'd rather not have.
They may seem irritating, counterproductive, or downright shameful. Never-
theless, they exist. Just as all the surrounding characters in your waking dream
are part of you, so, too, are all the characters within yourself. Whenever you
attempt to deny or repress any of these shadow selves, it only serves to add to
their power. That's why consciously accepting them, and providing equal time
for all their perspectives, is essential to the Fifth Invitation.

Let's say you've worked hard to establish a strong sense of independence.
You take care of yourself well, and purposely avoid situations that would
cause you to rely unduly on others. But then, you find yourself feeling suddenly needy. It may occur with a parent, boss, or anyone else from whom you
secretly wish approval. It may arise especially in a romantic relationship,
shattering your usual self-containment and leaving you exposed and vulnerable.

Before, if such a spell of neediness occurred, you might have shut it down
immediately. Now, you create the space and time for a proper internal airing.
You let your needy self take the stage all alone, without any competition or
criticism. You may find, in this process, that a little bit of attention is all that's
necessary to quell the sudden agitation. Or, once you're tuned in, there may
be more information revealed about why the neediness arose.

Shadow selves, indeed, can often see what the rest of you can't. In this case it may turn out that you need to speak your mind or make a change. If so, you don't have to do it in a needy way. Once it's been heard and acknowledged, your needy self will most likely recede. Then, a more steady and skillful self can take care of the rest.

You can't change your selves any more than your feelings, sensations, or impulses. But the more you make room for all your selves, the larger you're certain to grow. In the spaciousness created by this acceptance, your competing selves no longer fear annihilation. They begin to demand less and offer more, enabling you to negotiate between them like an enlightened referee. This kind of balance, obviously, can't be hurried or forced. It's what arrives, naturally, when you're no longer afraid of the dark.

Put down this book for a moment and pick up a pen. Finish the following sentence as many times as you can in one minute—"One of the worst things about myself is . . ." Don't look hard for your responses. Only write what arises naturally. These "worst" parts of you are your most easily identifiable shadow selves. To give them their due you don't have to wait for them to leap out and assault you. Do it right now just by naming and claiming them. *I have a judgmental self. I have a lazy self. I have a weak self. I have an insecure self.*

When you're done naming and claiming, take a big breath. Stretch your body and shake it out. It can be unsettling to own what you revile, but these selves are just a *part* of you. Your "best" selves are just a part of you, too. As they all come and go, ebb and flow, you remain. You're the dreamer. You're nothing less than the whole dream.

The most challenging shadow selves, by far, are the ones you can't name because you're not even aware of them. These aspects of yourself are so unacceptable or terrifying that they've been driven deep into your unconscious. You can't work with them, of course, till you know they're present. By welcoming all the shadow selves you do know about, however, you can create an environment that encourages the hidden ones to surface. In addition you can actively seek them out.

One way to conduct your search, using the method described earlier, is to play the characters in your life that bother you most. But if you're as committed as you are courageous, there's also a major shortcut. Whenever something aggravates you about another person, just assume it reflects a shadow self that's at least partially unconscious. The bigger a reaction it causes, the more unconscious that shadow self probably is.

If you absolutely hate rude people, take it as a sign that you have a hidden obnoxious self. If you can't stand people who express every little feeling, recognize the self in you that needs to let it all out. If you recoil at insincere people, be aware that you possess a phony self. At first, almost always, this practice produces a lot of resistance. You may insist that no such shadows exist within you. This type of defensive response is common, and will subside quickly if you're willing to continue. Once you locate even just one of these shadows, you'll be ready to appreciate each and every aversion as a signpost to a secret self.

Let's say, in your case, it's those insincere people who really get to you. At first glance you may see yourself as the opposite of insincere, always willing to speak your truth. But there may be something phony even in the way you respond to insincere people. Perhaps you mock them behind their backs, or smile through your teeth whenever they appear.

There's an important connection between unconscious selves and unconscious feelings. Sometimes claiming a shadow self will bring up waves of associated emotion. You might, if opening to a phony self, feel a lot of embarrassment and guilt. This process can also happen in reverse. You might, when opening to long-resisted embarrassment and guilt, uncover the phony self that's been laboring to conceal them. In order to understand this connection fully, it's helpful to review the First Invitation sections Triggers (page 26), Foremost Fears (page 29), and Difficult People (page 36).

If you've reacquainted yourself with these earlier passages and still have trouble accessing a particular shadow, try a simple experiment. By yourself, or with a supportive witness, act out the very trait you despise. For just a few moments, as an example, be as rude, expressive, or phony as humanly possible. Whatever quality it is you're seeking to summon, give this shadow play your all. It can often reveal what would otherwise elude you.

Remember, the goal of this investigation is not about good and bad. Nor is it about how you should respond to the world around you. Instead, it's about discovering and embracing yourself at a level far beyond comfort or convention. When you can love yourself that fiercely, that unconditionally, it's impossible not to love everyone and everything in the exact same way. The dream of your life becomes truly luminous, and the whole world is drawn to your light.

PORTRAIT: JUDGING

THE JUDGE

*B*renda is an engineer with a razor-sharp mind. She's only interested in personal growth and spirituality if it makes sense, if it appeals to her logically. When exploring her shadow selves at a workshop, she finally gave up in frustration and blurted out her truth.

"Y'know I get the whole dream thing—it's all about becoming more creative and expanded. But my whole life I've heard this idea about the shadow, that whatever you don't like about someone else is a reflection of yourself, and I have to say it just doesn't ring true for me."

I asked Brenda if she'd be willing to dialogue about it in front of the group. She agreed. That dialogue is reproduced here, without any additional description or commentary.

"Okay, let's begin: Tell me about someone who really bothers you."

"Sure. There's this commentator on TV. He's incredibly mean, overbearing, and most of all judgmental. I can't stand him."

"Are you ever judgmental?"

"Not really."

[Her sister interjects: "C'mon. Sometimes you are."]

"Yeah, that's true, but I work hard not to be. That's the whole point. It's not like I'm unconscious about it."

"Do whiny people bother you in the same way? Or greedy people?"

"No."

"So why do you think judgmental people really get under your skin?"

"Well . . . I think it's vile."

"So you have a judgment about it."

[The groups laughs] "Well, you got me there. I was unconscious about that."

"And if you judge the judge in others, you probably judge the judge in yourself. Maybe not a lot. But at least just a little. And whenever you do, it's bound to shut you down."

"Right. I can see that. So then what am I supposed to do?"

"Welcome the judge. Own it."

". . . Okay."

"Go ahead. Try it right now. Say, 'I have a judgmental self. I love it.'"

"That's hard. I don't think I do love it."

"Are you sure? Can you love it without liking it or acting it out?"

"Well, yeah. That I can do. Because it's a part of what is."

"Great. Now from that perspective, why do you think you sometimes judge?"

"Hmm. I judge someone when they don't respect or value me. Or other people."

"And how does it feel to be disrespected and unvalued?"

"It hurts."

"So sometimes you judge when it hurts. Is it possible that the commentator does, too? Is it possible that he judges a lot more than you because he hurts a lot more?"

"Maybe. I guess. But it's just as possible that he's mean by nature."

"Sure. We can never really know. But both are possible, right? So with that in mind, and without having to like or approve of the commentator at all, can you love him as you love yourself?"

"Umm. I get it now. I think I can."

LUCID LIVING

Clarity and strength of purpose are what
fulfill your heart's desire.

*H*ow much control do you have over your life? Some tell you that you create your entire reality. Others counter that virtually everything is predetermined. Still others suggest that your life is already perfect, and that you can experience that perfection with nothing more than a shift of view.

Most of us are interested more in practicality than philosophy. We'd just like to control our lives as much as possible, and are always on the lookout for new techniques. One of the best techniques, often overlooked, is derived from lucid dreaming.

A lucid dream is one that you're aware of while it's happening. This awareness allows you to influence the dream's direction, which many people believe can influence your waking life as well. To do so requires knowing where you'd like the dream to proceed, and then choosing the best course of action to get there. Say you're striving to work through fear, for instance, and have a dream about being surrounded by assailants. If you've trained yourself to be able to witness your dreams, then you might also be able to defeat the assailants one by one. The experience of a courageous victory in dreamlife might make it easier to find that same courage amid ordinary, everyday events.

Once you begin to live like you're dreaming, however, the nighttime step is no longer necessary. In other words, you can dream lucidly while wide awake. To begin, you must carefully refine your intentions. This can be more difficult than it sounds, because your many selves often have competing agendas. When you set intentions without enough unanimity, some selves will work toward them while others will work against them. If you've ever made a New Year's resolution only to break it a day or two later, you have a clear idea of how that occurs.

To avoid such a breakdown, your intentions can't be dictated by will. Instead they must be arrived at by committee. Not all your selves have to be thrilled about a particular direction, but each must have its say. One of your disciplined selves may institute a rigid diet, for example, but in order to get buy-in from a reluctant self it might need to establish a weekly free day.

Once you've surveyed all your selves and settled on a particular intention, you then need to bestow it with power. This requires no magic, complicated method, or secret of any kind. All that's necessary is enough awareness and conviction to support your intention with consistent action. With every supportive action you take the intention grows a little stronger. Conversely, with every opposing action you take, the intention grows a little weaker. Most intentions, even the loftiest, are realized through countless minute choices.

Start sampling the power of intention right now. Focus on one major intention. It might be something like *get a better job, exercise regularly, make amends with my parents*, or *find a healthy relationship*. Write down all the reasons why it's important to you, making the very best case you can. Next write down all arguments against it, letting every opposing self weigh in. See if you can negotiate a forward course of action that honors both sides.

Once you've done so, begin immediately. Identify one supportive action that you can take in the next hour. If you're working toward a healthy relationship, for example, a first action might be describing for yourself exactly what a healthy relationship is. Just that one simple step would bring vital energy to your intention. As soon as you've completed your first action, identify three actions that you can take tomorrow. Continuing with our example, these might include additional basic steps like determining where you'd have a good chance to meet an appropriate partner, what would best increase your own readiness, and putting actual appointments on your schedule to get started on both accounts. Before moving ahead, stop to feel how much strength your intention can gain from even the most incremental actions. Then, identify ten more actions that you can take in the next week.

Continue building in this way, action by action, choice by choice, and you'll be amazed at what happens. Things will often seem to fall in place all on their own. People, events, and circumstances will mysteriously appear to assist you. Your intention will become a great wave of possibility, re-dreaming reality with its irresistible force.

Despite all your progress, however, at times you'll likely get sidetracked. You may sabotage the process. You may minimize what you've already accomplished. You may become impatient and grasp at a quick fix. You may get discouraged and want to give up. Or, even though they all began on board, some of your selves may break rank and rebel.

Luckily, the path to renewed intention is paved with the first five Invitations. When you open to all your emotions, you're no longer compelled to act out. When you question your beliefs and opinions, you're unhindered by rigid thought. When you stop resisting the way things are, you're free to create them anew. When you welcome the specter of death, your life force can't help but surge. And finally, when you heed the wisdom of your unconscious, your many selves join together as one.

The more you master the power of intention, the more unified your waking dream becomes. You know exactly who you are, exactly where you're going. This inner harmony, if linked with the seven Invitations as a whole, makes you less susceptible to resistance of all kinds. It keeps you fluid, assured, and receptive. You feel more love than ever before, and with this depth of feeling comes an equal depth of understanding. You grasp the power of love to work miracles, even in the darkest lives and the gravest crises.

This realization leads you to embrace a new and overriding intention—to offer yourself as an instrument of love. Every lesser intention, when viewed from this perspective, either fortifies or falls away. As you begin to serve love, you inevitably serve others. Service to others, which in the past may have arisen out of duty, now becomes a great privilege. Reaching out to the hearts around you, and uniting with them, is what fulfills your own heart's desire.

ACCEPTING THE

FIFTH INVITATION

To the best of my current and evolving ability, I resolve to:

- Re-dream every mundane moment

- Make peace with my painful patterns

- Broaden my perception of the past

- View others as a self-reflection

- Revel in my array of selves

- Reclaim all my shadows

- Master the power of intention

THE SIXTH INVITATION

Love Like You're Dancing

Dance when you're broken open.

Dance if you've torn the bandage off.

Dance in the middle of the fighting.

Dance in your blood.

Dance when you're perfectly free.

—RUMI

In the Sixth Invitation, love calls you to

transform all your relationships into a dance

of self-discovery. When dancing together

in unison, through every step and stumble,

each partner reveals the other.

Setting your heart on fire changes everything. Instead of holding on for dear life, you dance with life. Open, energized, you find yourself gliding along effortlessly with life's ever-dazzling flow. Life and love become indistinguishable, washing away every one of your requirements for happiness and replacing them with the experience itself. Problems and challenges still abound, but they, too, take on an intoxicating glow.

In the wake of this transformation comes a desire to share it, to create personal relationships that are equally transformed. The Sixth Invitation is about how to accomplish this. It's about a new kind of relationship based on complete openness. This isn't the openness of clear and honest communication, although it certainly includes that. The openness we'll explore in the context of relationships is the same one we've been exploring all along.

When you're open to the present moment, and to the love that courses through it, you can join with another person at a depth otherwise impossible. Rather than bonding over shared interests, unconscious patterns, or mutual needs, you create partnerships based on celebrating one another's wholeness. Such partnerships are often dedicated to fostering greater love, not just between the two of you but everywhere.

Since most people find the greatest possibility for such sharing within romantic relationships, that's where we'll place the majority of our focus. But keep in mind throughout the exploration that much of it can be applied to other relationships as well.

Relationships are where most of us learned about love, and where we developed our understanding of it. They're also where we primarily still seek it. But our seeking often bears the marks of early conditioning and social convention. We pursue the love we know, even if it's distorted by misfortune or wounding. Then, if we're willing to grow, we concentrate on choosing healthier relationships, and on making ourselves worthy of them. Rarely, however, do we revise our conception of what brings love about in the first place.

Love, as the first five Invitations have made clear, is accessible at all times and in every situation. It's what bridges the heart of existence with your own personal heart. It calls you first to connect with yourself, and then to the world around you.

You might think, by this point, that applying these principles to relationships would be natural and seamless. Eventually it will be, but first comes the awkward process of supplanting old habits with new behaviors, and of reconceiving any limiting romantic beliefs. Though for a while it may seem like you have two left feet, everyone can excel at this dance.

Whether ancient or contemporary, precise or free form, dance is an expression of connection. It merges body, mind, and spirit into one movement, one moment. At its best dance can be liberating, ecstatic. Everything fades away except now, and now, and now. To love like you're dancing with an intimate partner requires the same degree of presence.

In the dance of love there are actually four partners—you, the present moment as you experience it, your partner, and the present moment as he or she experiences it. Your dance with the present is your own. The same is true of your partner's. If both of you are gliding along easily with the present, open to yourselves and to love, then you can follow one another's movements with grace. If either or both of you are shut down, disconnected from yourselves and from love, then the dance between you becomes immediately strained.

Understanding the nature of this quartet is crucial. When you're not available to yourself, you simply can't be available to your partner. Nor, in the same circumstance, can your partner be available to you. But usually we forget this. We make the majority of disconnections personal. We mistakenly believe that our own shutdowns are caused by each other. We become bogged down in assuming or denying responsibility, which only serves to shut us down more.

Keeping the four partners in mind puts an end to all this. It's like removing a thousand pounds of pressure. Whenever stepping on each other's toes we back off, take a deep breath, and reconnect to ourselves. Only when fully present do we join again. Or, we recognize and announce our own resistance, bring it to one another, and ask for help. We view the facilitation of one another's presence as the dance of love at its most sublime.

This approach applies to all stages of a relationship. To understand it better, let's begin at the beginning. Ordinarily, a relationship ensues when two people are lured together by the thrill of infatuation. In this heightened state they feel bigger, better, happier. They usually can't be bothered by an investigation of this state, which is often less about lasting love and more about make-believe. Then, when the onrush of infatuation fades, they're beset by a host of doubts. These doubts all center on one question—*Can we truly give one another what we want and need?* Struggling with such a question often leads to the kind of extreme stress that can doom a relationship right at the outset.

As you learn to fulfill your own heart's desire, however, you no longer expect others to do so. Nor do you seek to fulfill the heart of another, since clearly that's not your job. Freed from these impossible expectations, you're now able to evaluate a new relationship differently. Your focus can shift from future outcome to present experience. Rather than losing yourself in a swoon or shutting down with doubt, you can yield to the rhythm of the dance.

The steps of this dance are none other than the first five Invitations. These Invitations, when employed in a relaxed and delicate manner, can guide a couple through every relationship passage. They can ensure the greatest possible evolution, both for the union and the two individuals involved. To experience this in action, let's return to your hypothetical new relationship, allowing one moment of truth to stand in for the rest.

Suppose the relationship has progressed, and now you must decide whether or not to make a commitment. The decision isn't coming easily, and you find yourself almost equally divided between attraction and reluctance. You wonder whether all that reluctance is actually about the other person or just a result of your own issues. To uncover the truth, in this instance, would mean tolerating a period of frustration. It would mean forgoing the need of an immediate answer while you bring the first five Invitations to bear. Doing so would be slow and deliberate. You'd follow the instructions below like a waltz.

Inspired by the First Invitation, Feel Everything, begin with a survey of your attraction. Allow yourself to experience it fully. Pay close attention to its depth, breadth, and nuance. Let your attraction move through you, plain and simple, without attempting to understand, evaluate, or change it. Then, and only then, do the exact same thing with your reluctance.

Inspired by the Second Invitation, Question Everything, explore all your beliefs about this potential partner, about the current status of the relationship, and about how it will develop in the future. Examine your beliefs about what benefits this relationship may provide, and what it may require you to give up. Observe your beliefs about relationships generally, in all their forms, and which of those forms most suit you. With each line of questioning look for the underlying basis of your beliefs, and especially for any assumptions that may be faulty or premature. And wherever you discover assumptions that may not hold up, endeavor to stretch beyond them.

Inspired by the Third Invitation, Resist Nothing, list every single flaw in your potential partner. Without censoring or sugarcoating, include any feature or trait you'd like to change, improve, or perfect. Then, beholding them one by one, allow yourself to experience all the resistance they elicit. Notice where the degree of charge is low, moderate, and high. Where it's high, your response calls for further inquiry. This inquiry is vital to distinguishing between matters where you and your potential partner are basically mismatched, and matters that are really about self-acceptance.

Inspired by the Fourth Invitation, Live Like You're Dying, focus on your fear. Allow all your fears about this relationship to surface, and then let each one build to its fullest expression. Experiencing these fears will bring you, over and over, to the inevitable fear of death. With each repetition of this process your courage will grow and your fear subside. Of course, it's never so cut and dried. The actual experience is often painful and messy. Yet as a result you'll come to trust your final decision, knowing that fear isn't secretly behind it.

Inspired by the Fifth Invitation, Live Like You're Dreaming, assess whether this struggle over commitment includes a call to attention from your unconscious. Does it occur with most relationships? It is possibly a destructive pattern? If so, open to all the feelings it brings up. Follow those feelings to their source, to the events during which you first shut down. Move through any additional feelings still trapped there. This may open up a Pandora's box, and take more time than you hoped to invest. Stopping anywhere short of your goal, however, will keep you a prisoner of the past.

Once confident that you're free of the past, continue to draw upon the Fifth Invitation and revisit the list of your potential partner's flaws. This time, investigate how they reflect your own. Don't leave any flaw on the list until completely clear about what it highlights in your shadow. Creating this one-to-one correspondence might feel like a game at first, but there's nothing more important. To see another clearly you must first see yourself clearly. Often, when you do, many of your potential partner's seemingly insurmountable flaws quickly diminish in importance.

Finally, in drawing upon the Fifth Invitation, solicit your entire range of selves for their viewpoint on the current crossroads. From the most prevalent to the most shadowed, let all your selves have an uninterrupted say. When they're done, you're done.

Does all of this seem overwhelming? A little more like plodding than dancing? This can stem from having it laid out in sequence, when with practice it becomes much more fluid. In addition, a decision about commitment is a major turning point. Sustained intimacy, by contrast, takes root over countless minor moments. These everyday experiences require a subtler, lighter touch. After all, relationships are intense enough. There's never a reason to add intensity.

And yet, in one key way the Sixth Invitation *is* demanding. It requires that you surrender routine in every aspect of relationships. To remain enchanting, the dance of love can never feel rehearsed or predictable. Any commitment, once you decide to make it, must be continually renewed. When each day of your life is alive with the decision to stay or leave, nothing is ever rote. Staying becomes as electric as your first date. And leaving, too, if it's the best option, can occur within love's embrace.

For as long as a partnership prevails, its very existence is an invitation, a vehicle to become all that you are. But it's also an occasion to grow beyond yourself, to serve your beloved's unfolding in the same way you serve your own. To love truly, in any relationship, is to place the ultimate fulfillment of another above the onslaught of your momentary needs. While it's not your responsibility to provide that fulfillment, you're certainly the best one to encourage it. Furthermore, there's no such thing as a selfless act. By offering attention, support, and reflection for a blossoming partner, you bestow yourself with the resulting bloom.

ILLUMINATING THE

SIXTH INVITATION

Love turns one person into two,

and two into one.

—ISAAC ABARBANEL

SHALL WE DANCE?

*The evaluation of a new relationship needs to
happen in its own rhythm and time.*

*A*nything new, by definition, is unknown and unformed. It hasn't had the chance to grow, to clarify, to reveal all its subtlety, splendor, shadow, and surprise. The dance of relationships is especially like this. When it's just beginning, partners are often clumsy. They haven't learned how to move together, how to stay connected to themselves, the present, and each other. Dreams aside, they can't yet be sure of themselves as a couple. That's why, at first, the single most important ingredient is patience.

Patience in a new relationship means staying focused on the current moment, letting it breathe, without crushing the present in a wave of "what if?" When a relationship is difficult and confusing, and patience seems impossible to come by, that's when it's more important than ever.

A key aspect of patience is the trust that everything will be revealed in its own time. In other words, whatever you can't tell about a partner or a partnership usually isn't yet knowable. Pressuring for premature clarity can stop a relationship before it ever really starts. It can also keep you from seeing and savoring what *is* present.

Why such an accent on this natural unfolding? Because resistance to it is so common, and causes so much undue pain. It can happen whether you're hopeful about a relationship or wary. If you're hopeful, there's often a fear that your partner isn't. This creates a tendency to probe, to press. Even when handled delicately, it can still set the whole affair on edge. If you're wary about the relationship, there's often a fear of losing control. This creates a tendency to retreat, to shut down. And as long as you're not fully present, there's no real relationship to evaluate.

To exercise patience when hopeful, wary, or any combination of the two is certainly a challenge. You're likely to ask, *How long is long enough?* The answer is that your body always knows. Your body is where the steps of any new dance need to click. It's where you can actually feel whether you're suitably partnered. When you've gathered enough information and experience, such knowing will resound with clarity.

If you don't yet have such a knowing, let your body communicate what it does know. This can help you find the deepest source of your uncertainty, and cut through the repetitive chatter of resistant thought. Thoughts like *Maybe he isn't emotionally available* and *I'm not sure she really gets me* can rarely be debated to resolution. When you ask your body to weigh in, however, you'll always get a quick "yes," "no," or "not sure." You might not want to accept the answer, but that just means there's resistance to work through.

You may also ask, *Isn't trying to remain patient in the face of mounting anxiety the same as shutting down?* The answer, in this case, is yes and no. If you try to act patient while feeling the opposite, that's definitely the kind of shutdown that only make matters worse. On the other hand, anxiety is not actually a feeling. Anxiety is the fear *of* feeling. Therefore, returning once again to your body allows you to find that fear and open to it.

Then, once the fear settles, you can feel what you've been girding against. It might be, for example, rejection. Accepting the possibility of rejection, which exists at every moment of every relationship, would provide two immediate benefits. First, it would eliminate the cause of your initial fear and anxiety. Second, it would induce a calm in which patience can thrive.

In real-life situations, this movement from anxiety to patience is rarely a one-time proposition. For a while anxiety may keep arising. Its source may stay the same or change. Relying on your body alone may lead the way to acceptance, or you may also need to employ refocusing and inquiry. Even so, it may take numerous rounds of opening before a lasting calm arrives. But with each round you'll become a little more patient, and regain a little more access to love.

If you're not in the early stage of a romantic relationship, there are most likely other new relationships to explore with this perspective. You may be wondering, *Should we go into business together?* or *Should we become roommates?* Practicing patience, and relying on the emotional truth of your body, can be invaluable in situations like these. It's what keeps you connected, aware, regardless of what you can't yet know.

VARIATIONS ON A THEME

Recurring issues provide a

healing opportunity.

S ay you're at a party, surrounded by dozens of attractive people. Out of the whole crowd, one person catches your eye. It seems like there's a lightning bolt between the two of you. Conversation ensues, during which it feels like maybe, finally, destiny has brought your beloved.

Soon, a full-fledged romance begins. Things are intense, yet also somehow calm. And then, in bits and pieces the truth emerges. Your partner has a serious immature streak, hasn't really grown up, and in fact hungers for parenting as much as partnership. This revelation is a stunner, since your own romantic history has included far too much caretaking of others and you vowed never to make the same mistake again. The whole thing feels like a giant cosmic trick. You want to run away, hide, give up on love altogether.

But this supposed cosmic trick is actually nothing of the kind. It's not a crisis, a warning, or a backslide either, even though conventional wisdom may regard it as all three. Instead it's just a theme, a dance of dependency, in which you and your partner are perfectly matched. In fact, if you cut off contact abruptly and seek a more appropriate partner, chances are the same theme will just recur in a different guise.

Every relationship has at least one main theme. All partners find themselves dancing the same steps over and over to the same disconcerting refrain. You can recognize a theme by the charge it carries, by its power to dance *you*. For both partners a relationship theme contains the key to greater wholeness. It's as if love is saying—*Look! Here! This is where you need to heal.*

In the above example, if either of you were truly done with this parent-child theme it wouldn't have shown up. And if you don't take advantage of the opportunity to heal through it, but struggle to make the relationship work anyway, the theme will tag along like a third wheel for the whole journey. Time and again you'll find your partner clingy, selfish, and draining. Time and again your partner will find you cold, distant, and nagging. The more each of you struggles to repair the other, the more bitterness and resentment will reign.

If you're drawn to an overgrown child who needs serious nurturing, it's because there's a part of you crying out for the same. Your opportunity in this relationship is to acquaint yourself with the needy child in you, and to bring that child in from the shadows once and for all. If your partner is drawn to the security of a parental figure, it's because the internal adult has been banished or underdeveloped. Your partner's opportunity in this relationship is to answer every bout of habitual childishness with a genuine step toward self-reliance.

Though this parent-child theme is certainly common, it's just one among many. There's the push and pull between solitude and togetherness, intellect and emotion, and control and abandon. In their description these all seem like pairs of opposites, but in actual relationships no one remains entirely at either extreme. You may take the parental pole in some issues but feel more like a child in others. Your partner, rather than coming across as all child/no parent, may instead seem more like sixty/forty.

Because we're all made of many selves, a relationship may contain a number of main themes. They might even overlap or contradict one another. You may prefer solitude when it comes to your free time, for instance, and wrestle with a partner who craves more sharing. During sex, on the other hand, you might be the one craving connection while your partner prefers more distance.

While themes usually show up as problems, that's not always the case. You may enjoy expressing lots of emotion and rely on your partner for a more composed approach. This division might suit your partner, too. But if such an arrangement keeps either of you from connecting with your whole self, it's a theme worth exploration. Whatever you can't connect to in yourself you also can't share with your partner. Your love, as a result, is limited.

You and your partner might be prone to pleasing each other, to take another common theme, and think the arrangement works just fine. But how many selves must be excluded in serving one another so diligently? How long until they emerge from the shadows and exact their price?

If you're currently in a romantic relationship, pause to identify its main themes. If you can't tell just by looking for a charge, investigate the roles you commonly play with one another, as well as the way you divide your daily responsibilities. Ask your partner to do the same, but don't share your lists until they're complete. When you do share, be careful. Sometimes just naming a theme, whether it's on one list or both, can create a sudden burst of friction. There's no reason to disagree about whether a theme really exists. As long as one partner feels it, at least to some extent the theme is real.

If you're not currently in a romantic relationship, pursue the same investigation regarding a past partner. Or review an ongoing relationship that's important but nonromantic. All relationships have themes, and each theme is an opportunity for greater opening.

Whenever you find a theme, the next step is indeed to open. Reclaim any aspect of yourself that you've unconsciously foisted on another. Reconsider any role, no matter how seemingly beneficial, in which you find yourself shutting down. Give yourself plenty of time, months even, and use all first five Invitations to help. That means feeling, questioning, and accepting. It means letting death infuse the process with vitality, and dreaming yourself ever more whole.

To explore this process in greater detail, let's return to our earlier example of the new relationship, which is beset by a troubling parent-child dynamic. Since in this example you're the one overidentified as the parent, you'd begin by focusing on the aspect of your partner's childishness that upsets you most. Perhaps, as is common, it's money. Perhaps your partner unintentionally bounces checks, causing the electricity to get turned off or the phone to be disconnected. While your friends may say, "Run for the hills," and eventually you might, your first task is to stop to feel everything.

At first it may seem as though you're just frustrated and angry, but if you stay with those feelings they may yield to an underlying fear of chaos and helplessness, of an overall loss of control. Opening to the fear of those experiences, and then allowing yourself to actually feel chaotic, helpless, and out of control would reveal how long such feelings have been denied. If you've been carrying them around unconsciously for many years, they would have had no other choice but to draw your attention with a painful life pattern, as described in Repeat Performance on page 149. This parent-child theme, indeed, might be just such a pattern.

But now that you're no longer repressing these states, and are willing to feel your own chaotic and helpless emotions, you'll no longer be lured to partners who so fully embody them. Or, if your current partner was willing to explore the dynamic separately, from the other side, the two of you might be able to share notes and support one another. You might be able to grow more whole together. Either way, having served its purpose, the pattern can finally come to an end.

When you're unsuccessful in accepting difficult emotions like helplessness, once again refocusing and inquiry become invaluable tools. Refocusing prevents you from shutting down amid lots of negative charge. Inquiry helps you challenge any core beliefs that may be providing that charge with power.

Often, even when the process of acceptance seems to be moving right along, significant fear reemerges and stops everything cold. Letting that fear escalate to its full expression, and welcoming your imaginary demise, can liberate hidden reserves of determination. So, too, can playing your partner's role in this dream. Imagining every nuance of your partner's childishness, and feeling them as if they belonged to you, might be the last step in reclaiming all you've disowned. Far from the comfort of your take-charge persona, you might discover a shadow self that's surprisingly immature and dependent. Even if you knew it was there before, and intellectually accepted this, now you'd have the chance to express it from the inside out.

Sometimes, when both partners open with such courage, a theme disappears. Other times it continues to appear, but without any of the previous drawbacks. There's no harm in remaining the more mature one as long as it doesn't make you invulnerable. There's no harm in remaining the more childlike one as long as it isn't a barrier to responsibility. And one final, important note. Even if your partner shows no initial interest, and you're the only one opening, the relationship is still bound to change. The love you liberate eventually may bring the two of you closer, or it may highlight how you've danced apart.

PORTRAIT: CUTTING LOOSE

"*T*his all sounds like so much work! Forget it! Love is about joy and sweetness and coming together to be better than you could ever be apart. That's what *I* want. Not just to love like I'm dancing, but to dance because love makes me so happy I can't help but dance!"

After Kate's outburst, an expectant silence filled the hall. What would happen next? Would she leave in a buff? Would an argument break out? Instead, somebody chuckled. Then somebody laughed. Then suddenly everyone was laughing, even Kate. She had voiced a feeling we almost all feel from time to time, one that was lurking beneath the surface of the whole workshop. Now that it was out, the mood became freer. Real exploration could take place, and Kate actually volunteered to begin.

She had been married for seven years, and was about to file for divorce. Her husband Paul was deeply spiritual, but not at all interested in what he called the "mundane" details of daily life. He could talk about his emotions more easily than most men, but would rarely make the bed, take out the trash, or remember to pick up the eggs. This left Kate to do all the "un-fun" stuff, and filled her with resentment. She wondered, as her opening proclamation made clear, when it would be her turn to dance.

When asked to label the primary theme in her relationship, Kate came up with "doing versus being." She longed to do less and be more but felt trapped, since she wasn't willing to live in a pigsty or go hungry. Kate's being side was a shadow self. She was painfully conscious of it but didn't see a way to reclaim it.

The first important step was just to feel her being self. When was the last time she had? "Well," she told the group, "Probably a few minutes ago when I shot my mouth off." And what was it like? "After the tension broke I was all warm and beaming. Kind of like I *was* dancing. Wow, it's been so long since I actually danced." Would she be willing to dance right now? "But there's no music." Someone pointed to a CD player in the corner. "In front of everyone? No way."

After some more discussion, Kate agreed to take the CD player back to her cabin and dance there by herself till lunch. After lunch, she gave a report.

"You know," she said, "A few times I had to stop dancing because I was crying so hard. They were happy tears, though, like I was finally back in my center. I kept thinking, *This is me! This is me! I need this in my life.*"

Realizing that it wasn't an all-or-nothing proposition, Kate spent the rest of the afternoon working out a plan. Devoting three nights a week to this place of being felt just about right. Maybe she'd meditate, do yoga, or Jazzercise. She'd put all relationship decisions on hold for now and would watch what happened. This wasn't for the marriage, though, she wanted to make clear. It was for her.

Checking in about two months later, Kate was distraught. "I didn't know it back at the workshop," she said, "but I had a secret desire that my decision would somehow change Paul. Like in all the books, I thought if I focused on myself then he would feel the change in me and magically start to focus on *himself.* Instead, when I come home from yoga the house is even messier. I feel like I reunited with that sense of being in myself, and now I just want to be somewhere else."

Hearing herself, Kate had to laugh. Being, she began to see, isn't something you can put on your to-do list. It may feel wonderful, even essential to stretch and dance and meditate, but the real task is maintaining that sense of being while *accomplishing* the to-do list.

What would it be like to take out the trash as a dance? To shop for groceries as a dance? Even if Paul *never* did his fair share? Now Kate had a real adventure ahead of her, and was heading into totally uncharted territory.

"I'm like a fourth grader at this," she reported a few weeks later. "But I'm making good progress. And here's the main thing I'm seeing—when I love my life like I'm dancing, then I can love Paul like I'm dancing. And that really makes him stand up and take notice. Whether or not we stay together, I feel like *I'm* getting it together."

STOP THE MUSIC

Relationship triggers can bring
love to a halt.

You can't give or receive love when you're shut down. It's that simple. And yet the people you love the most are also the ones who trigger you the most. And the people who love you the most are also the most triggered by you. Of all the reasons that relationships are confounding, this has to be near the top of the list.

Triggers, as we discussed on page 26, are comprised of the people, events, and situations that cause us to shut down routinely. Each of us has a unique set of triggers. Each of our bodies shuts down uniquely as well. Take a moment to review the way your own body registers a shutdown. Do you experience a racing heart, pressure in the diaphragm, shortness of breath, or all the above? Most of the time you're triggered, the ensuing shutdown happens in the exact same way.

Triggering can happen in relationships whenever you don't get what you want. Your partner does or says something "wrong" and down you go. The more the same thing happens, the more power the trigger accumulates. The deeper the emotions that get stirred, the trickier it is for you to recognize your shutdowns and reopen. If your partner often forgets to pick up groceries, as in Kate's Portrait, the first few slipups probably won't even shut you down. By the hundredth time, however, the resulting trigger might be overwhelming.

When you're triggered, the fight-or-flight mechanism is activated. Forget about dancing—you're practically climbing the walls. All you can focus on is making the sensation go away. You're combative, defensive, self-blaming, or any combination thereof. Your heart may beat wildly, but it's closed. Whether or not you say a word, such an animal state is communicated nonverbally, energetically. And except in rare cases it will elicit the exact same state in your partner. The harder you press one another for a particular response, the less likely you are to get it. It's like an endless game of tug-of-war in which nobody can get the upper hand.

All this adds up to one thing: it's a mistake to discuss any delicate or vital subject when triggered. It only makes matters worse. Even when both of you stay calm and rational on the surface, the tug-of-war still functions beneath. Even when the buildup of so much tension leads to a cathartic breakthrough, it can come at the price of hard-earned security and trust.

The obvious solution is to recognize whenever you're triggered and stop the interaction cold. Yet to do so takes rare composure. The animal state is so overpowering that it usually shuts off your access to higher functioning. The only way to become adept at trigger spotting is by continual practice. At first it may take hours to regain full awareness. But soon you'll whittle that down to minutes, and eventually just moments. No matter when it happens, though, as soon as you can say to yourself, *I'm triggered*, you can also say it to your partner. You can break the cycle of increasing tension by simply asking to step away and regroup.

In fact, it's helpful to have a standing agreement about this. That way, as soon as either of you share that you're triggered, the conversation automatically stops. When that's impossible for whatever reason, both of you still know to tread very lightly. Since triggers bring out the worst in us, this approach can be fundamental in protecting any relationship. Choosing temporary emotional distance, and the safety it provides, is a way for you and your partner to act lovingly toward each other even when one or both of you feels the opposite. It may be a while before your hearts fully soften, but rarely will anything else get them there faster.

Another aid in working with relationship triggers is knowing them in advance. Make a list of everything about your partner that often shuts you down. Ask your partner to make one also. Too neat or messy? Too talkative or quiet? Since triggers are automatic, and you're not responsible for them, nothing is too petty for the list. Squeezes the toothpaste from the middle, chews too loud—if it shuts you down, write it down. Remember, this isn't about how to deal with any of these issues. It's only about when *not* to deal with them.

Make a list, in addition, of the topics and situations that frequently get to one or both of you. Money, sex, politics, religion, in-laws, and care of the kids are obviously common, but every relationship also has triggers all its own. Placing an issue on the list, of course, doesn't mean you shouldn't talk about it. But whenever you do, try to keep on trigger alert. With enough practice you'll be able to spot a trigger up ahead, before it's too late, and avoid a shut-down entirely.

Whenever a trigger cannot be avoided, just a ten- or fifteen-minute time out is all it takes to open and drop down to a deeper emotional experience. Though challenging, this opportunity is available even if you have the quickest temper or tend to go stone cold. And if you see it all the way through, your resulting choice of words and delivery will be as compassionate as possible. Your partner will be the least likely to get triggered in return, and might actually feel closer to you than ever.

TWO TO TANGO

Beneath the urge to fight lies

much to uncover.

Many people who embrace the path of love see conflict as its opposite. They avoid conflict as much as possible, especially in romantic relationships. But real conflict, beyond the instinctual response of triggering, can actually be an instrument of love. It's one of the best ways to access the theme of a relationship, and to heal what that theme brings to light.

Conflict arises in a relationship, just like triggering, when you're not getting what you want. The natural response is to fight for it, or to manipulate the situation to bring it about. If your partner makes a hurtful comment, you might make a stand for greater sensitivity. If your partner spends too much time away from home, you might find things around the house that demand attention. Of course you also may simply act out periodically, denouncing your partner in an inappropriate way. But in these cases, too, the basic principle is still the same. You want something, you're not getting it, and therefore the peace is disturbed.

To focus immediately on what you want, however, is to miss everything a conflict has to offer. It requires closing off from what's happening within and placing too much emphasis on your partner. This rarely feels good. It works even less. Even if your partner is tolerant, or sorry, or vows to shape up, the resulting release of tension is as temporary as it is superficial.

When a war dance has broken out, and you aim to restore a more lasting peace, what's called for is introspection. To ensure that this introspection is direct, daring, and not just an intellectual exercise, it must make use of all the

Invitations. This point is crucial, because it's easy to get lost in popular ideas about the differences between men and women, or the role of varying personality types. While such information can be useful to explain emotions, or manage them, it does nothing to help you *feel* them.

Feeling, first and foremost, is what's required. You've probably heard about the importance of using "I" statements when discussing difficult interpersonal issues. There's no question that starting a sentence with the words "I feel" can help create an open and safe environment. But in order to use such statements successfully, you already need to be feeling. Or, more precisely, you need to have been feeling long enough to distinguish between passing flashes of reactive emotion and the deeper feelings tied to a relationship theme.

Let's look at a hypothetical scenario in which you embrace a relationship conflict in order to heal and grow. Suppose you're having dinner with friends. Right at the table, in front of you and everyone else, your partner begins flirting with another guest. Your first reaction is absolute shock. For pride's sake you bite your tongue, but immediately begin rehearsing a tirade for later. *How dare you flirt like that, and right in my face! You're rude, selfish, and totally without class. What do you think that makes* me *feel like?! A piece of dirt, that's what. Do you care about me at all? I mean why am I even asking—it's obvious you don't.*

Instead of unloading like this, however, you realize that you've been seriously triggered. Turning to your body, you notice a rapid heartbeat and a shortness of breath. These are two of your signature shutdown signs. As you open to them, they gradually begin to ease. In their place appear all the feelings you instinctively had tried to avoid—rage, jealousy, and humiliation. Keeping quiet, you open to these feelings as well. Even in the car, when your partner senses a problem and asks about it, you just say, "Yes, there is something going on, but I need a little more time alone with it."

Over the next day or so, as you remain open, those initial emotional responses begin to fade. You find yourself feeling lonely, most of all, unmet in the tenderness and caring you bring to the relationship. This taps into a theme of pursuit-withdrawal, with which you're already quite familiar. It's been a pattern over the years for you to choose partners who don't love you back. For months, in this current relationship, you've been settling for far less connection than you crave. And now, each time you acknowledge that lack of connection, it hurts a little more.

The hurt returns you to early wounds stemming from the absence of parental love. You know that as long as you don't allow those wounds to surface fully, you'll continue to repeat the same pattern. Finally, after so much stalling, you allow yourself to stay in the pain of those wounds for long stretches of time. This hurts, too, but it also heals.

To help the healing along, you expand the memories related to it, applying the process described in The Big Picture, on page 152. This includes not just seeking additional context for your wounding, but also playing the role of whichever parent was involved. Reimagining the event from that parent's vantage point helps you bring compassion to the healing process. While such compassion is initially directed at the parent you play, in time it naturally widens. You come to experience this same compassion for yourself. Soon, even though there's likely to be additional healing required, you feel calm and whole enough to share with your partner.

Only now, what you have to reveal is light-years away from what would've poured out that night. It might go something like this: "When we were out to dinner, it seemed like you were flirting. I was really angry at first, but then I figured out why it bothered me so much. For a while now, I think, I've been more invested in our relationship than you. That's nobody's fault, but it's also not healthy for me. I'm wondering if there's a way for us to become more balanced."

Following along with this scenario, you may have encountered serious doubts. You may wonder if all that introspection is necessary. Perhaps there's nothing wrong with the relationship at all, and your partner just needs to wise up. Or perhaps you're the one who needs to wise up, having blown the situation totally out of proportion. Even if both were true, however, what you discovered beneath the surface is also true. The theme is at play. The healing is real. The war dance is over, at least your own participation in it. This enables you to begin dancing once more with the present, connected to yourself and to love, whether or not your partner is equally free to join in.

A SAFE DISTANCE

Clear boundaries help loving

relationships thrive.

Try the following experiment. Ask a friend to stand across the room and then approach you slowly. With each step, notice how your body responds. If the distance between the two of you continues to feel safe and comfortable, allow your friend to keep going. But the moment it feels unsafe, and your body rebels, tell your friend to stop. Right then, notice where and how your body gives you the signal. Once that's clear, tell your friend to back up. When your sense of safety is reestablished, pay attention to where and how you know that, too.

Your body, as this experiment makes clear, is how you register your sense of personal space. When your personal space is broached against your will, your body may suddenly feel like a suit of armor. If you try to bring someone closer than you can actually handle, your body may suddenly feel like a straitjacket.

Personal space is not just physical, it's emotional as well. Emotional space is commonly referred to as boundaries. In relationships these boundaries play a vital role. A healthy sense of boundaries marks a clear distinction between your own inner reality and your partner's. It means that you can love without losing yourself. An unhealthy sense of boundaries means that you and your partner have become overentwined. You may accede to your partner's needs and demands when it's not in your best interest. You may give yourself away, as explored in the Mine or Theirs Illumination on page 126.

When two dancers remain in a tight embrace, their movements can become constricted. Cheek to cheek is lovely at times, but oppressive if required at all times. By holding on to an ideal of lockstep partnership, many couples unnecessarily limit their dance. They mistakenly assume, even if it's unspoken or unconscious, that total fusion will heal all their wounds and fix all their flaws. In the process of clutching so urgently at one another, as well as at this impossible dream, they lose all ability to establish a safe distance when necessary.

Sometimes, surprisingly, more closeness is actually created by distance. In the space that partners open up for one another, they often find themselves moving independently in new and more expressive ways. This is true in relation to having separate interests and friends, as is routinely acknowledged, but it's also true in relation to one another's emotional life.

The dance of love, remember, is a quartet. Each partner dances first and foremost with the present moment. It can be as satisfying to witness and support a partner's ongoing dance with life as it is to leap headlong into one's own. In addition, occasionally dancing together while purposely far apart makes a whole new range of connectedness possible. When partners grant each other the room to let loose, and then embrace each other's most expansive uniqueness, their union correspondingly grows.

You don't need to develop the capacity for well-defined emotional boundaries. As the above experiment demonstrates, they're innate. But you may, as many people do, need to stop ignoring the messages your body sends. This isn't always so easy, and can require significant reorientation. If you've become used to living in the state of alarm that boundary crossing creates, that alarm may now blend into the background.

Repeat the boundary experiment again, only this time in your imagination. Replace the friend with your current or most recent partner. Before beginning, conjure up one of the most precious memories between you, when the two of you felt enchantingly close. Once you're basking in the memory, imagine your partner walking toward you. Let them keep walking unless your body protests. Most likely, it won't. Your partner will probably end up in your arms.

Now repeat the experiment one last time. Before beginning this round, conjure up one of the worst memories between you, possibly a time of hurt, anger, and bitterness. Imagine your partner walking toward you until your body says, "Stop." Where does it happen—twenty feet, ten feet, five feet? There's no right answer, of course, because every person and situation is different. But any sort of triggering or conflict is almost certain to extend your boundaries outward.

Even the closest relationship dance, if it's healthy, is about the *interplay* of union and separation. Consequently, boundaries change constantly according to the present circumstance. Boundaries are also influenced by the past. Someone with a history of emotional violation may need more space in the same situation than a person whose relationships have been basically safe. This need may lie dormant for long stretches and then resurface without warning. In a moment of sensual pleasure, for example, when the need for separation feels nonexistent, an innocent comment, a sudden memory, or merely the brush of a hand can flood such a person with overwhelming emotion. It may take time and distance to integrate, or even just to plumb the mystery.

To honor your boundaries with a partner means learning to give them a clear voice without succumbing to guilt or pressure. Only fear can keep you from succeeding. By now you know both ways to move through fear, but here's a quick refresher. As described in Emotional Flow on page 23, you can find its physical location and then open to it, allowing the fear to rise and fall unimpeded. Or, for a more difficult but lasting approach, as described in Beyond Fear on page 132, you can magnify it into the resistance of death and then proceed from there. Once you've completed whichever type of opening feels more appropriate, the final step is to give yourself all the physical and emotional space your boundaries need.

To honor the boundaries of your partner means granting him or her the same degree of physical and emotional space whenever it's requested. It means creating the kind of supportive environment that *encourages* boundaries to be invoked. In fact, attending to boundaries on a regular basis is what makes true support possible. Without knowing where your own emotions leave off and those of your partner begin, any attempt at support is likely to bog down in confusion. You'll either assume that your own feelings belong to your partner, or assume that your partner's belong to you. Fortunately, when the ownership of emotions becomes clear to both of you, all such confusion is easily avoided.

All this talk about the necessity of respecting boundaries may lead you to feel powerless. *What if my boundaries are so extended that they make intimacy impossible?* you may wonder. *Or what if that's the case with my partner?* The silver lining with regard to boundaries is that the more they're honored, the more they soften. Even in the most extreme cases, it's just a matter of time and intention before prohibitive boundaries begin to recede. On the other hand, your boundaries may be a common trigger for each other. When one of you needs space the other may take it personally, reacting with isolation or aggression. In this case your boundaries may wrench you farther and farther apart. Only by feeling your way through the triggers, and healing what they conceal, will you be able to bring this cycle to a halt.

In what areas of a relationship might you most often ignore your boundaries? Do you ever feel too enmeshed in work, play, sex, family responsibilities, or daily activities? In what areas might you most often ignore or resent your partner's boundaries? When you feel like you know the answers to these questions, share them with your partner and ask for feedback.

To love authentically in any relationship requires that you become adept at assessing and heeding your boundaries. But it doesn't call for you to overemphasize them. Too much vigilance around boundaries can render you brittle, unnecessarily guarded, and less available for intimacy than ever. That's why it's advisable to test your boundaries often.

Avoiding any undue force, make it a habit to coax yourself gently toward a greater degree of closeness. Such growth is often uncomfortable. At first it can feel very similar to a real boundary violation. Give yourself lots of practice, therefore, to distinguish between the two. If your discomfort diminishes within a few minutes, it's about growth. If your discomfort remains or intensifies, you're pushing too hard.

Because the difference between boundary coaxing and boundary violating is often subtle, let's pause for a moment to consider both. Suppose you love to cook, and the kitchen has always been your private domain. You make a grand mess and enjoy every minute of it. Your partner's more fussy and methodical style is therefore unwelcome, except when it comes to washing the dishes. But lately it's occurred to you that such an arrangement creates a little more separation than necessary. So you talk to your partner about it, focusing on your fears around cooking together. These fears may include being criticized or controlled, or even just having to adjust to another person's flow. The two of you decide to prepare one meal in tandem and see how it goes, checking in with each other every once in a while. Such an experiment, with its obvious consciousness and care, is the epitome of gentle boundary coaxing.

But now suppose the experiment proceeds badly. It's virtually untenable to have your partner so close. Even though nothing is being said or acted out, you can feel your partner yearning to do things differently or straighten up after you. You're not sure whether it's real or projected, but you can also sense a strong judgment about your whole whirlwind manner. Before the main ingredients are even laid out, you want to scream and call the whole thing off.

What to do? Of course the choices are many. You could take a time out and talk it over. You could give up for the night and order out. You could divide the kitchen in half, thereby creating a small comfort zone. But as long as the tension escalates without the slightest sign of relief, it would be a mistake to continue the experiment as planned. Rather than softening your boundary it could backfire, causing you to snap like an overstretched rubber band.

Keeping the difference in mind between coaxing and violating, which areas of your relationship call for more intimacy? Where are you most ready to encourage it by testing your boundaries? What new aspect of your inner sanctum are you willing to share? What new aspect of your partner's inner sanctum would you most like to share? Discuss these questions when the time is right. If you're both open, and respectful of your boundaries throughout the discussion, it's almost certain to strengthen your bond.

DANCING IN THE DARK

Sexual shadows can either

enslave or enlighten.

Pleasure, for the most part, is a sensual phenomenon. You gaze at a river with your eyes, inhale its scent through your nose, hear its roar with your ears, feel its surface with your hand, and taste its flavor with your tongue. Even the most mental pleasures, like a precious memory or a leisurely daydream, reach their fullest expression in the body. It's impossible to capture any moment of joy, to really feel it, without an outer or inner smile.

Sexual pleasure, however, is often more complex. A longtime partner's touch, though applied just the way you like it, may still grow to feel numbly familiar. To experience your most intense sexual heights, you may find yourself adding the spice of fantasy or risk. In addition, the power of judgment can be severe. When what stimulates you the most is considered wrong, by you or anyone else, pleasure becomes a highly charged proposition.

What you bring into the sexual arena is nothing less than all that you are. Often, in fact, what's repressed in every other aspect of your life finds its release in sexuality. That explains why powerful people can be so drawn to masochism, or powerless people can take refuge in sadism. The Sixth Invitation shies away from none of this. It makes no preference between gay or straight, sweet or rough, kinky or run-of-the-mill.

To love like you're dancing in the sexual arena means doing whatever safe and consensual activities you enjoy. But it also goes far beyond that. It's an opportunity to explore your sexual response as yet another way to open more fully to yourself, the present moment, and your lover. This isn't easy to do, however, because when the topic of sex is involved, the dance can become feverishly intense. Your blood races, your heart pounds, and the beat grows more insistent. The thrill of it all can overtake you, diminishing your powers of attention and leaving you oblivious to any deeper meaning. That's why from time to time you need to step back and reflect, separating not just from the dance's beguiling rhythm but also from your own desire.

Suppose, for example, that you frequently fantasize about sex as a member of the opposite gender. For a man, this may signify a yearning to express his receptive self. For a woman, this may signify the desire to embrace her assertive self. How would you know if this applies to you? Paying attention to the fantasy's lure, you'd identify what about it provides the greatest arousal. In other words, what turns you on is always an arrow to the truth.

The more you pay attention, the more specific the insight. A man's receptive fantasy, when explored in depth, might be a call for emotional presence. It could also, just as easily, demonstrate a need for spontaneity. A woman's assertive fantasy, when explored in depth, might be a call for clarity of intention. It could also, just as easily, demonstrate a need for self-reliance. All these instances present the same opportunity—to let the energy of the sexual fantasy pervade life's nonsexual aspects as well.

Let's walk through an example of this process in a little more detail. Imagine finding yourself drawn to sexual situations and scenarios in which you express a lot of hostility. This might be as troubling as it is exciting, especially if you consider yourself a placid person. To begin exploring it, you'd attempt to feel the raw hostility itself, and all its energy, apart from sexual expression. If you found yourself blocked by judgment of the hostility, you'd question this judgment with the Shades of Gray exercise beginning on page 54. If you found yourself blocked by fear of the hostility, you'd once again enlist the help of Emotional Flow (page 26) or Beyond Fear (page 132).

Then, when there's nothing left between you and your hostility, you'd combine the First and Fifth Invitations in a slightly new way. This would entail stepping into the "role" of the hostility as if it were a person. The goal would be to hear its entire message, loud and clear. You might want to write it out, shout it out, or even dance it out. Any of these approaches that seem suitable, either alone or in combination, would allow you to reconnect with a part of your emotional core.

You might learn that this sexual hostility is a call to stop denying your hostility in general. But often the correlation isn't so direct. The hostility might be fueled by old and unacknowledged wounding. Right in the middle of your journaling, shouting, or dancing, suddenly tears of hurt and sadness might flow. Shifting your role play to align with the shift in feelings might bring about a much needed release and a very different message. Behind all your belligerence, in such a case, could be a surprising need for more tenderness and self-care.

Sometimes, when you're willing to embrace sexual healing this way, what used to arouse you now loses its power. Other times that power diminishes only slightly or not at all. The point isn't that what turns you on is ever good or bad, right or wrong. It's merely a display of fireworks, lighting up the path to self-discovery. However far you travel on that path remains completely up to you. But keep in mind that many intense emotions and deep wounds have a way of becoming sexualized. Exploring your sexual behavior and fantasies, as illustrated above, may be the only way to know they're present.

If you've spent years getting free of shame, struggling to allow yourself a form of sexual expression that's truly satisfying, you might be reluctant to explore your desires in this way. Likewise, if your greatest pleasure is *connected* to shame, if it feels the best because it's forbidden, you may not be willing to lose the rush. Again, there are no rules. But from the standpoint of the Sixth Invitation, the question is always this—does your chosen form of sexual expression lead to more love or less? Or, put another way—are you willing to trade a particular sensation for the chance to open your heart?

Without pressure or judgment, search your sexual desires for those that might trouble or confuse you. Are there any desires that you fantasize about excessively? Are there any you've never shared? Is it possible that keeping these desires to yourself is also keeping you separate from your partner?

This is, of course, very delicate territory. The sharing of sexual secrets always has the potential to trigger one or both partners. But even if it does, the story doesn't have to end there. Hopefully, as discussed in Stop the Music on page 193, you and your partner have gained the tools to work through triggers whenever they arise. Most important among these tools is the standing "time out" agreement. As long as either of you remain triggered, there's no benefit to continuing this type of conversation. But once you've taken the time to become fully present, it's possible to share sexual secrets in a way that enriches you both.

If your partner has flirted right in front of you, to continue with our earlier example, you might simply ask, without fear or rancor, "Is there anything between us that you haven't brought to me yet?" Your partner, if committed to the same type of inquiry, might move through guilt and apology to respond in kind, "I think there is something bigger going on. The flirting was just a symptom. I've been craving more sexual adventure lately but didn't know how to ask for it. I was worried that you'd say no, or would think there's something wrong with me."

Since partners are rarely compatible in all ways when it comes to sex, it's possible in this situation that you might indeed say no. But there's always a greater chance for loving connection when a couple's sexual desires are out in the open. It's not about fulfilling each other's every fantasy and need, but creating a safe space in which to communicate them. Without such open communication, neither of you can know for sure what each other's response will be. You're unable to negotiate, let alone experiment. Ironically, this most intimate aspect of relationship is usually where communication first breaks down. When communication goes, so goes the pleasure. This often leads, as compensation, to forms of acting out like withdrawal or affairs.

In your partner's above admission about flirting, the surface conduct and underlying issue were both about the sexual arena. But as previously explored, that's often not the case. Your partner might just as likely respond, "I think this is about my weakness with boundaries. I feel hemmed in and need to spend time alone. I didn't realize this until I found myself pushing you away with all that flirting, but now that it's conscious I'll be much more responsible."

Disclosing your sexual shadows, whether they're solely about sex or extend beyond it, can be even scarier than sharing vulnerable emotions. That's why, perhaps, the above exchanges may at first seem unrealistic. But the Sixth Invitation necessitates a radical and fearless honesty, especially in regard to sex. You don't have to like everything in your partner's sexuality, or participate in it, but you do need to accept it. If you're not accepting, you're resisting. And here, just as everywhere else, resistance cuts you off from yourself, the present moment, and love.

Desires arise on their own. You can't control them any more than emotions. Rather than acting out or repressing them, however, you can always explore and convey what they reveal. Inevitably, your willingness to share the depths of your sexual psyche, and to bear loving witness to your partner's as well, is what revitalizes the physical aliveness between you. In the aftermath of such primal revelation, the immediacy of a common touch becomes incredibly heightened. The very act of breathing becomes unbelievably erotic. To receive one another with such sweeping presence, as both animals and angels, is to dance with transcendent grace.

TRADING PARTNERS

The dance isn't really over until

you've let love lead.

Why have a partner in the first place? Historically, the primary reasons were social and economic. Love, if present, was a lucky fringe benefit. Then, over the last century, the idea of partnership transformed completely. We still demand the security of a working family unit, but now also require deep, ongoing intimacy. Since either can be all-consuming, many relationships collapse under the pressure.

The pursuit of therapy and other forms of personal growth can often, unintentionally, add to this no-win situation. It's possible to vow, defiantly, "I must get my needs met once and for all. I won't settle for anything less." Then, when a partner falls short, there's no choice but to leave or suffer. Many people strive mightily to heal, to awaken, only to find themselves pickier and lonelier than ever.

To love like you're dancing creates a bridge between the need for perfect union and the impossibility of ever finding it. That bridge, as we've seen, leads ever inward. When there's a problem with your partner, you focus first and foremost on yourself. In so doing, you flow from blame to responsibility. When you're not getting the love you want, you use the first five Invitations to keep dancing with the present moment. This grants you access to the love that's *always* present, whether your partner is or not. By opening your heart and tapping into this love, you flow from resistance to acceptance. While this may seem to condone hurtful attitudes and behaviors, in practice it does the opposite. By accepting your relationship just as it is, you're able to stop contributing to or exacerbating what ails it.

Every time you opt out of a negative pattern with your partner, you inevitably change that pattern. Your own freedom to act differently sets the stage for your partner to act differently. Often, without a word of prompting, you recognize shifts in your partner that previously seemed unimaginable.

But what about when that doesn't happen? What if you rise to meet every one of love's challenges and your partner stays intractably stuck? In such cases you must recall the highest purpose of partnership. It's not to satisfy one another, although satisfaction is a powerful lure. It's not to share your burden, although sharing is surely required. And it's not to comfort one another, although comfort is a great blessing. The highest purpose of partnership is simply this—to serve one another's opening to love.

This service cannot be provided when your partner feels judged, accused, condemned, or attacked. But neither can it be offered when you coddle your partner, becoming a silent accessory to suffering out of your own frustration or fear. The middle way through these extremes is to let love speak through you, to offer love's Invitations as a humble and supportive ally. These Invitations, whatever the issue that prompts them, are best tendered in moments of relative calm. They often begin with heartfelt, personalized, more informal versions of the following questions:

THE FIRST INVITATION:
FEEL EVERYTHING

"Is there anything you may be feeling about this but haven't discovered yet? If I were in the same situation, I might feel . . ."

"Whenever this topic comes up, I notice you get a little tense. Does it bring up any feelings you'd rather avoid?"

THE SECOND INVITATION:
QUESTION EVERYTHING

"It seems like you have a lot of strong beliefs about this. I'm sure I do, too. Would you be willing to look at our beliefs together?"

"I'm not certain you understand what I'm saying. Could you tell it to me in your own words?"

THE THIRD INVITATION:
RESIST NOTHING

"You're being really hard on yourself. Is there a way you could approach the situation without as much criticism?"

"You're being really hard on me. We may just see this differently. Can we accept that about one another?"

THE FOURTH INVITATION:
LIVE LIKE YOU'RE DYING

"What's really most important to you in this situation? At the deepest level?"

"Does the choice you're considering feel right for *you*, or is it more about someone else's expectations?"

THE FIFTH INVITATION:
LIVE LIKE YOU'RE DREAMING

"It seems this same problem keeps cropping up in different ways. Do you think anything might underlie the pattern?"

"You sound pretty sure about this. Are there any parts of you that feel differently?"

THE SIXTH INVITATION:
LOVE LIKE YOU'RE DANCING

"Do you feel triggered right now? Would it be helpful to continue this later?"

"We've been arguing about so much lately. Can we look together for the deepest reason?"

Take a moment and reread those questions. Imagine how you might feel if someone presented them to you. Chances are, if there was even a remote possibility of letting down your guard, such entreaties would support the process.

Take another moment and read the questions once more. Imagine them spoken in a clear, caring voice, without the slightest trace of presumption or superiority. On the one hand, they do nothing but softly convey love's call. On the other hand, they may be the very difference between the end of a relationship and a thrilling renewal.

Not only do questions like these often bear fruit right away, but they also plant powerful seeds. Sometimes these seeds need time and space to grow. Today's fervent denial can become tomorrow's sudden breakthrough. This month's angry rebuff can become next month's gradual thaw.

On the other hand, staying present doesn't mean waiting forever. Though no relationship is beyond love's healing, in some cases an actual departure is first required. When the time to depart is close, you'll have a clear knowing. This knowing won't be in the form of thoughts or impatience, but will arise as the physical guidance we've touched on many times before. When you ask whether it's time to leave and turn your attention to your body, rather than a "no" or a "maybe," the response will be an unmistakable "yes."

Even so, if you leave to escape your own issues or to evade the discomfort of growth, it's difficult for the necessary healing to take place. Therefore, whenever you're about to give up on a partner, ask yourself one last time, *Have I fully accepted my role in our theme? Have I taken responsibility for my part in our conflicts? Have I done the work on myself that love requires?* If the answer to all these questions is also yes, then you're ready to move on to the next dance.

ACCEPTING THE

SIXTH INVITATION

To the best of my current and evolving ability, I resolve to:

- Let new relationships unfold in time
- Detect each love's major themes
- Stop arguing whenever I'm triggered
- Find the root of every conflict
- Honor relationship boundaries
- Explore my sexual shadows
- Serve my partner's opening to love

THE SEVENTH INVITATION

Widen Your World

The One is none other than the All,

the All none other than the One

—SENG TS'AN,

THE THIRD ZEN PATRIARCH

In the Seventh Invitation, love calls you to

see the earth and its inhabitants as one

interdependent whole. To serve and sustain

that whole means assessing the global impact

of all your actions.

*W*hen you walk the path of love, your embrace of true partnership applies not just to lovers but also to family and friends. You relate from the heart as a moment-by-moment practice, seeking to inspire the same in your entire circle. Your intent expands beyond that circle as well, including everyone with whom you interact. There's no waiter or gardener or banker or street person who doesn't merit a lasting look in the eye and a sincere, heartfelt connection.

But what if the *whole world* were your partner, including the billions of people who inhabit it and all the resources on which they depend? What if every single one of your actions either honored that partnership or disrespected it?

What if the world was even more than a partner? What if it were a vast extension of yourself? What if every single one of your actions affected you directly?

The Seventh Invitation affirms that the world, indeed, is both partner and self. This isn't just a poetic flourish but rather a precise description. You can find its confirmation everywhere, from the nature of subatomic particles to the function of your own body to the law of supply and demand.

Let's look first at subatomic particles. Scientist who explore this quantum domain have known for many decades that every object in the universe is composed of the same primeval dust. A dog, a jet, a virus, and a bottle of beer—they're each made from remnants of the big bang. To say we're all one, from this perspective, is less a spiritual principle than a simple observation.

But out of this observation comes an unexpected discovery. Two sub-atomic particles that once interacted will still respond to each other's motions eons later, even if they've traveled light-years apart. As to why this happens physicists can only conjecture, but one thing is definitely clear—distinct and far-flung elements can influence one another in extraordinary ways.

Is this true beyond the subatomic level? Can you influence the course of events with thought, for instance, or prayer? While the debate about these questions rages on, the interconnectedness of all matter is something you can *feel*. Love, not surprisingly, is what enables you to tap in. The more you love, the more you experience yourself as united, fundamentally, with all of existence. To whatever degree you can influence the course of events, this union is what makes it so.

While no one can actually see what transpires at the subatomic level, much of how your own body functions is perfectly visible. At first glance it seems that you maintain basic control of your body. You tell it when to eat, sleep, and exercise. You decide what kinds of remedies are best for it. You determine when to push it to the edge of its abilities, just as you choose when to let it relax.

This initial vision of your body is misleading, however, because of all it leaves out. There's your genetic code, which largely predetermines an array of features such as size, complexion, personality, and lifespan. Then there's the whole series of bodily processes that happen automatically, such as digestion and metabolism. In addition there's your body's permeability. You have little ability to filter pollutants from your breath, keep microbes from your membranes, or avoid toxins in your food.

For better or worse, all of our bodies are globally linked. Examples of this interconnection abound. When the deadly chemical dioxin is released in a faraway factory, for instance, it can drift into the atmosphere and travel thousands of miles to your neighborhood. It may end up in your body via rainfall or seafood. Tragically, it tends to concentrate in breast milk. A prosperous mother in a gated community, with the best of intentions and the healthiest lifestyle, may still poison her child unwittingly whenever it's time to nurse.

What does the brutal legacy of dioxin have to do with love? Plenty. To live in accord with love means you're willing and able to recognize how the world impacts you, and how you impact the world. And that recognition brings us to the law of supply and demand.

Suppose that this dioxin-producing factory we're discussing is in China, as many are, and that it makes action figures of Hollywood heroes. Most buyers are halfway around the world, here in the United States, and they want their action figures cheap. Because labor costs in America are relatively high, domestic companies can't produce the action figures at the price consumers demand. To succeed, these companies must contract with a foreign factory, such as the one in our example, which faces fewer workplace and environmental regulations, and therefore routinely contaminates its workers.

Do you really want all this on your mind the next time you're a buying a child a gift? Probably not, any more than you want dioxin in the child's bloodstream. But to turn a blind eye to either reality is to ignore your own role in the equation. If you, and millions of consumers like you, were willing to pay more for dioxin-free action figures, they'd be on the shelf of your local toy store within weeks.

This may sound like activism, yet it's really just a description of how the world works. Interdependence is both pervasive and constant, at every level, even when it's difficult or disturbing to see. To widen your world means even more than just recognizing this interdependence. It means making all your choices, both little and large, with an eye toward enhancing the greater whole. If there were a simple formula for doing so, then the Seventh Invitation would be easy to accept. Unfortunately no such formula exists, which makes this last Invitation the most challenging of all.

At first, when you recognize how much power your actions truly have, it can seem like nothing but an opportunity. Just as one plume of a chemical can spin the world off balance, one loving visit to a nursing home can ease scores of aching hearts. There can be great satisfaction in sharing such love, not just with people but also with animals, insects, plants, and the very earth itself.

Then, inevitably, this initial enthusiasm dims. It happens when you come face to face with the unfathomable depth and extent of the world's suffering. Lives everywhere are wrecked constantly by natural forces like floods, earthquakes, and disease. Even more people suffer from man-made causes such as hunger, poverty, war, oppression, and crime.

If you're like most of us, encountering so much pain with such an open heart could quickly cause you to go numb. *If I'm supposed to feel the whole world's struggles on top of my own*, you might protest, *forget it. I'll just become incapacitated and useless.*

This type of numbness, just like the numbing ideas we discussed earlier, is an overly protective reaction. To feel the whole world's struggles *would* be debilitating, but that's why love doesn't require it. Love only asks that you don't turn away, that you bear witness to suffering wherever it exits, and that you learn to meet it with compassionate action.

Even when you're willing to do so, however, there are five additional types of resistance to global suffering that can often still arise. Before reviewing them, let's pause for a moment to consider that phrase, "resistance to global suffering." At first it sounds like something positive. After all, isn't global suffering unwanted? Shouldn't we seek to alleviate it? The answer to both questions, of course, is yes. But resistance, as we've been using the term throughout and will continue to use it here, means a rejection of something that exists. Striving to eliminate suffering has none of this resistance in it. Refusing to face that suffering, on the other hand, or allowing it to keep you disconnected—from yourself, your heart, your loved ones, the present moment, and the world at large—is exactly the kind of resistance that is debilitating both to you and the planet.

You cannot experience love for, or act in a fully loving manner toward, any person or situation that you resist. In addition, as we saw in the Third Invitation, trying to make positive changes while locked in resistance is virtually impossible. With that in mind, now let's look at the five forms of resistance to global suffering one at a time.

The first form of resistance is bitterness, an inability to accept so much darkness in the world. Condemnation of the world's darkness leads to withdrawal and passivity. Almost always, however, such condemnation stems from discomfort with one's own darkness. When personal shadows are fully welcomed, the world's shadows can be welcomed as well.

The second form of resistance is futility, the conviction that suffering has always been and will forever be a part of life, and that trying to effect change is just a waste of time. Futility is more about frustration than actual fact, in light of all the positive changes—such as the end of slavery, women's rights, and wheelchair access—that we've now come to take for granted. Opening to frustration over how hard it is to make change happen, and how much change still needs to happen, usually causes the sense of futility to diminish.

The third form of resistance is denial, the decision, typically unconscious, to retreat into a life of privilege. When surrounded by so much wealth and opportunity, it's easy to pretend that the rest of the world is too. This denial is actually encouraged by affluent countries. To maintain the status quo, these countries need their citizens to consume without conscience. Mainstream media helps ensure that they will (see Why Do I Want What I Want?, page 63). By remembering to Question Everything, however, especially the values of popular culture, it is possible to opt out of this cycle.

The fourth form of resistance is fear, a concern that opening fully to the world's sorrow will necessitate a surrender of freedom, individuality, and the ability to live a full life. Many people are also afraid of surrendering comfort and convenience, whether in the everyday products they use or the luxuries they enjoy. What all these fears tend to obscure is that love doesn't call for any one type or degree of sacrifice. Each of us is always free, no matter how open we become, to follow the lead of our own hearts.

The fifth form of resistance to global suffering is overwhelm, a dizzying uncertainty about how best to help the world or even where to begin. Since there are so many issues, so many sides to each issue, and an endless supply of information, compassionate action can seem best left to experts. When the mind doesn't know what to do, however, the heart always does. By listening to our hearts we learn where our greatest passions lie, and therefore on which issues we're most suited to focus. We find the courage to get started, to take small steps, to make mistakes and become the stronger for it.

How many of these types of resistance seem familiar? Have you experienced them in combination? Do they often function beyond your awareness? The Seventh Invitation is about bringing them to light and diminishing their grip. It's about refusing to partake of the global bounty—food, clothing, shelter, natural resources—without finding a way to give back.

Resistant or not, you're a citizen of the world. Opening to that resistance means taking your citizenship seriously. It means committing to serve the world wherever it serves you. If your shoes are manufactured in Samoa, then to an extent you're Samoan. Whatever benefits those shoes bring to the island are partially due to you. Likewise, however, any sickness, poverty, or environmental degradation they cause is also partially due to you. The same is true of your Korean stereo, your Mexican bookshelf, and the Nigerian cocoa in your favorite candy.

Be aware, as you read this, of any new resistance that wells up. Numbness, bitterness, futility, denial, fear, overwhelm—are any of them suddenly present? Is there a part of you that wants to reject so much responsibility? If so, don't fight it. Just pause to feel everything that arises. Welcome even the most resistant thoughts. Breathe, reconnect with your body, and let all your reactions peak and subside.

Once you've released your resistance to suffering, in all its forms, it can actually become a blessing to widen your world in this way. It inspires a hunger for real understanding, a desire for more than simplistic sound bites. This leads you to broaden your perspective with an array of views that may be unpopular, marginalized, or even suppressed. It readies you not just to learn but but also to act. Such actions might be safe, like boycotting an irresponsible company, or they may be risky, like committing civil disobedience to oppose an unjust government.

Some people come naturally to this kind of action, but for others it can initially seem uncomfortable. *I'm just not political*, you might think, *that kind of thing's not for me.* What frees you from such blocks is understanding that there's a political dimension to everything. Politics is simply about power, how it's acquired and applied. There's politics in the jungle, on the playground, and whenever people gather in God's name. Politics are at work whether perceived, acknowledged, denied, or ignored. The last thing love wants is for you to shrink from any aspect of your own power. Rather, it wants you to bring that power to its fullest and most effective expression, guided not by need or self-interest but by what seems best for the entire collective.

Even then, however, sometimes your efforts will fail. For all your power and determination, the candidate won't win, the bill won't pass, and the species won't escape extinction. Or, unwittingly, sometimes your efforts may backfire. You may succeed in closing down a polluting factory, for example, only to learn that hundreds of the factory's employees could not find new jobs. These distressing realities plague anyone who attempts to serve the world with an open mind and heart. What allows you to persist in spite of them is the love that motivated you to serve in the first place.

Love is patient. In surrendering your sense of urgency, you recognize that lasting change can take decades. Often, a short-term failure may be just what's necessary to spur a final triumph.

Love is humble. In surrendering your need to have all the answers, you view setbacks as opportunities to learn. Everything, from specific tactics to your entire mission, is always subject to careful review.

Love is active. In surrendering your desire for certainty, you see that doing something is always better than doing nothing. The risks of succumbing to doubt, of letting hesitation turn into paralysis, far outweigh those of taking a stand.

Love, above all, is unconditional. In surrendering your attachment to an outcome, you find that widening your world is its own reward. You do what you do, beyond the hope for success, because it's an expression of who you are. When faced with insurmountable odds, or even certain defeat, there's no alternative but to keep following your heart.

Now take a momentary pause. Reread the last four paragraphs. But this time, imagine that they refer only to your personal life. In that context, most people have far less trouble adopting such a stance. Why? Because they feel more comfortable concentrating on themselves, and their own actions, than they do steering the world at large. "The best way I can change the world," they're prone to proclaim, "is to work on myself."

This common proclamation leaves out the other half of the story. One of the best ways to work on yourself is to work on the world. In doing so the deeper truth reemerges—the two are separate facets of a united whole. Your unity with all of creation now translates into concrete deeds. Working to better the world is what makes the world feel more like home. It's how your heart heals, grows, and ultimately ignites.

ILLUMINATING THE

SEVENTH INVITATION

One day when I was sitting quiet . . . it come to me: that feeling of

being part of everything, not separate at all. I knew that

if I cut a tree, my arm would bleed.

— ALICE WALKER

HOME ALONE?

Your private abode is
a global project.

*T*he sun rises. Your eyes flutter open. You loll a while in bed. They say that your home is your castle, and this morning it sure feels true. The rest of the world is far, far away. Or is it?

Now is the perfect time to bring the Seventh Invitation to life. Since you're still in bed, let's start there (feel free to adjust the following details as necessary). The Egyptian cotton of your comfy sheets comes, of course, from Egypt. The bedside rug was made in India. The hardwood beneath it was logged in Canadian forests, milled in Japan, and then shipped back across the Pacific for final processing in factories along the Arizona border. The varnish on the floor is a petroleum distillate made from Iraqi oil, shipped across the Atlantic to a refinery in Virginia, and then sent by train to a plant in Indiana for finishing.

Similar journeys were made, from resource to refinement, and from one continent to the next, for your nightstand, lamp, dresser, curtains, and most of the clothes in your closet. When it's time to get up, you slip on some of those clothes and head for the coffeemaker in the kitchen. The coffeemaker itself is another international endeavor, as well as its brew and your favorite mug. If you down a few supplements to start the day off right, they, too, contain ingredients from far and wide. In addition your breakfast plate, silverware, and favorite jam may have been imported. It's as if, just by shuffling from one room to the next, you've circled the globe a dozen times.

Global beginnings of even greater intricacy are true of your phone, com-

puter, and television. And your car in the garage includes worldwide compo-
nents too numerous to mention. All of these objects require a cast of thousands to arrive at your home. For starters this cast might include farm
laborers, factory workers, investors, accountants, salespeople, managers, re-
ceptionists, distributors, and salespeople.

This is interdependence at its most immediate and practical. It means that
you're never really home alone. While modern living generates more interdependence than ever before, it can also foster the illusion of self-sufficiency.
Seeing past this illusion is an essential element of love. It allows you to connect with distant lands and people that might otherwise seem inaccessible.

Followers of almost every faith are accustomed to saying grace before each
meal, to blessing the divine, natural, and human energies that went into its
creation. Once you recognize that the same energies are necessary for most aspects of daily life, you might be inspired to say constant grace. This outpouring of gratitude might be silent. It might come as acts of kindness rather than
words. Regardless of its form, the practice of gratitude is a surefire way to
open your heart. In fact, gratitude and love are closely related. Each one, over
time, can't help but create more of the other.

COMPASSION

A courageous heart never excludes.

Most people are basically kind. They're touched by the suffering of others. In the wake of disasters an outpouring of money, supplies, and support is certain to follow from all around the world. But then, just as certain, the outpouring dries up. Regardless of whether help is still needed, for the most part it's no longer available.

Why does compassion wane? The main reason is that it's difficult for us to have feelings about what we can't see or hear. When disasters happen, for a few days or weeks our TV screens are filled with the victims. We look into their eyes, hear their stories, and almost instantly begin plotting our assistance. As life goes on, however, different stories dominate the airwaves and our attention gets diverted elsewhere.

A related element in our declining compassion is proximity. Often the farther away something happens, the easier it is to forget. Starving children in Rwanda are rarely uppermost in our minds, while a starving child on our doorstep would demand immediate and constant focus. News programming plays a large role here as well. On the one hand it brings us closer to the plight of distant people. On the other hand it tends to sensationalize and trivialize the connection. This is true of local news as well. Whether near or far, traumas and tragedies float through our living rooms in a way that makes them appear more remote than ever.

The Seventh Invitation takes both these obstacles into account. It asks, however, that you do everything in your power to transcend them. When suffering exists that you can't see with your eyes, the aim is to look with your heart. When separated from those in need by real or seeming distance, the task is to imagine them as guests in your home. Native American wisdom counsels that a loving and reverent point of view should always include the welfare of seven future generations. As the world grows ever more interconnected, it's now just as important to consider the inhabitants of all seven continents.

Another barrier to compassion is self-interest. When someone else's trouble appears to threaten our own well-being, we may instinctively shut it out. We may perceive a threat to our money, family, property, community, lifestyle, or survival. In these cases, although we might be able to see, hear, and even touch people's suffering directly, none of that matters. Think of efforts to increase diversity in the workplace, for example, and how much harder they become to support when our own opportunities for advancement are impacted. Consider the "not in my backyard" phenomenon, in which people recognize the need for a power plant or waste facility but won't allow construction anywhere near their own neighborhood.

Threats to our religious, social, and political allies can also cause us to close our hearts. If we take a strong position in support of Israel or the Palestinians, for instance, it becomes more difficult to acknowledge the ordeals endured by the opposing side. Even when no allegiances are involved, and all that's at stake is our opinion, the same dynamic still comes into play. Ardent law and order advocates can have a hard time feeling sympathy for victims of police brutality, while civil rights proponents can downplay the perils that police officers face.

Reading this, you may think withholding compassion in all these cases is appropriate. You may protest that simultaneously fighting and feeling compassion for an adversary is both ill advised and impossible. While it's certainly not what most of us have been taught, or how most people operate, this approach is indeed possible. In fact, it is the only true path to harmonious and sustainable coexistence. Those who win without compassion almost always feel secretly superior. Those who lose without compassion almost always nurse a volatile resentment. In neither case can love bring the winners and losers together. The truces and settlements that result are rarely lasting or secure.

On the other hand, loving the people with whom you clash, even while detesting their positions, creates the opportunity for mutual respect. In such an environment all parties can gain from one another, and have a stake in forging a durable alliance. Furthermore, this approach remains preferable even when your opponents want no part of it. Without having to give an inch, or letting down your guard, you uphold the possibility of reconciliation.

The Second Invitation, Question Everything, cautioned against taking a particular side in any dispute if you're unable to recount the other. Now the challenge, beyond just recounting, is to step back from the fray whenever your compassion fades. This means temporarily ceasing to fight for any position until you can once again find a place in your heart for those you oppose.

Assess the limits of your compassion right now. Ask yourself who, if anyone, is unworthy of it. Those you conflict with religiously, socially, or politically? The people who hurt you the most, or wish you the most harm? Or perhaps a drug addict, rapist, child abuser, murderer, or terrorist? Remember, as you ponder this list, that the definition of compassion is loving care. It doesn't mean that the recipients haven't done wrong to themselves and others. Nor does it deny that they may have committed hideous crimes, deserve serious punishment, or even death according to some. In other words, it is possible to condemn people's actions with all your might and still feel compassion toward them.

Compassion, like forgiveness, cannot be rushed or faked. The lack of it commonly signifies great waves of anger and hurt, either currently surging or locked away. If you find it impossible to have compassion for any individuals or groups, but are willing to have that change, what's necessary is to move through *all* your feelings. Sometimes it helps, in this process, to imagine yourself face to face with the offending parties. Speak your truth, scream it if necessary, without regard for civility or political correctness. Keep coming back to your own feelings—*I'm so furious! I feel betrayed! My heart is breaking.*—so that rather than making accusations or judgments, instead you release your own pain.

If that doesn't open your heart completely, there are two more steps to try. First, picture these people as newborns, as toddlers, as students on their first day of school. Were they unworthy then? What unspeakable horrors must have befallen them between childhood innocence and adult depravity? Even if you believe in pure evil, and that monsters are born rather than made, what must it be like to bear such a curse?

Next, if necessary, use your ability to role play (page 155) and dream yourself inside the individual involved. If it's an entire group you're still hardened against, imagine yourself as a representative member. Then, try to experience the situation from that angle. It's not the person's beliefs or justifications that matter, but how it *feels* to live that particular life. If suddenly you're awash in hatred, try to touch the awful wounds that motivate it. If you encounter a complete lack of feeling, try to imagine a whole lifetime so frozen and vacant.

To widen your world, at its essence, means loving when it's hardest to do so. It requires a heart so huge that there's room enough for everyone and everything. Any wavering of compassion, either for those close to home or in nations far away, signals that there's work to be done. Heeding those signals, and doing that work, is the hallmark of a liberated life.

PORTRAIT:

SEEDS OF PEACE

No global issue is more deep or complex than the struggle between Israel and the Palestinians. Just mentioning the struggle usually brings up intense feeling and equally intense resistance. Middle Eastern violence can seem endless, hopeless, far beyond the reach of love and compassion.

But that's not how it looked to John. The son of Holocaust survivors who narrowly escaped death, John grew up feeling lucky to be alive. He went on to become an award-winning journalist, writing numerous books about the Middle East. His Judaism could easily have led him to see the region through biased eyes, but he wouldn't let that happen. The cynicism of his profession could easily have rubbed off on him, but he wouldn't let that happen either.

In 1993, John went to a Washington, D.C., cocktail party attended by the Israeli prime minister, the Egyptian ambassador, and a PLO representative. Suddenly, John stood up to make a toast. He began talking about how children were the only hope to break the cycle of violence. It sounded innocuous, perhaps a little simple, and then he caught the room off guard. John asked all three leaders if they would arrange for fifteen or twenty kids to come to a summer camp in the United States and learn conflict resolution. Embarrassed, cornered, one by one they all said yes. The next day, before they could backtrack or change their minds, John announced the camp publicly. He called it Seeds of Peace.

That first year there were forty-five campers. In the years since, the camp has grown to nearly five hundred. Its scope has expanded to include not just children from the Middle East but also from most other war-torn regions.

Each summer, camp begins the same way. Teenagers arrive angry, desperate to assert the righteousness of their cause. But they're also scared, facing the "enemy" up close for the first time, often wondering if they'll be stabbed in their bunks. In the days that follow, the campers swim and canoe and play sports together. They also meet for daily "coexistence sessions," in which they get to express their feelings and also learn to listen. Everything is fair gaine. Nothing is oversimplified or whitewashed. Frequently the campers lash out at one another.

"You lie to us!"

"We want our land!"

"Your bullets killed my baby sister. I was there!"

"Your suicide bomb murdered my friend. He was visiting his grandmother!"

There's plenty of shouting, and even more crying. Along the way it becomes clear that no one has a monopoly on either truth or suffering. Meanwhile, campers compete against one another in groups, with each group containing children from both sides of a conflict. In the process these rivals learn to collaborate, and even begin to trust one another.

When their sessions end, the campers face grave challenges. They return home to regions filled with enough hatred, violence, and oppression to make Seeds of Peace seem like an idealistic mirage. But they're also able to stay in touch with one another over the Internet, and sometimes even reconvene to hold their own summit talks. Over two thousand strong, Seeds of Peace graduates are both the beneficiaries and the embodiment of compassionate action.

Recently, skeptics pointed to the worsening Middle East crisis as a sign that such efforts have been useless. John fervently disagreed. He explained that the camp was a haven for emotional detox, a priceless end in itself. He created it primarily as an opportunity to promote love, which had always been his deepest motivation.

While the other portraits in this book rely on pseudonyms to protect their subjects, in this case there's no need. Though I never had the privilege of meeting him, the subject is well known. His complete name is John Wallach. His loving and determined spirit exemplifies the Seventh Invitation. He died of cancer at the age of fifty-nine, shortly before this account was completed.

FIRST, DO NO HARM

Loving the world begins with
daily decisions.

*L*et's return, while continuing our discussion of compassion, to your morning cup of coffee. A major export item of many poor countries, coffee's usual form of production causes two main problems. First, the crop is grown on plantations owned by gigantic conglomerates. These companies often pay near-slave wages to the local peasants who do the bulk of the work. Second, corporate coffee plantations require deforestation and heavy pesticides. This harms the local environment and threatens species of both plants and animals.

Luckily, alternatives exist. Many enterprising plantation workers have begun farming small plots of coffee, joining together in cooperatives, and selling their harvests to buyers all around the world who agree to pay a satisfactory price. This coffee, as you may know, is referred to as "fair trade." You can find it in most health food stores and even in one large international chain. Some of these same peasant growers are also reintroducing organic farming and biodiversity into their fields, which provides an opportunity for endangered species to repopulate. This type of coffee is called "shade grown," and is also widely available.

Every time you buy another pound, there's a choice to be made. For an additional few cents you can purchase fair-trade, shade-grown coffee, supporting this more just and sustainable approach, or instead stick with a conventional brand. Such a description may sound black and white, but daily life, of course, never is. Perhaps you're partial to an old-style, supermarket coffee, or shop in a store with limited options. You might forget about the issue from time to time and just buy what's handy, or even, having done your own research, come to an entirely different understanding.

Love and judgment don't mix. Therefore, this exploration is not about right and wrong. The coffee you drink, the clothes you wear, the car you drive—wherever freedom flourishes, these decisions remain yours alone. Compassionate action, however, requires that you make such determinations not based solely on preference, convenience, or budget, but also with regard to your worldly role.

Before beginning to practice, physicians take an oath. It includes the maxim "First, do no harm." The Seventh Invitation calls for the same oath. And when modern life makes some degree of damage unavoidable, your goal is to harm the least.

Since two or more sides exist to every story, how do you select the least harmful alternative? You question everything, resist nothing. This ensures that your viewpoint isn't distorted by unfinished personal business. It allows you to gauge the bias of others, whether clear or covert, and in the end trust your own conscience.

But what about the time and energy required for hunting down and sifting through so much information? Only a saint, you might protest, would continually go this extra distance. Only someone independently wealthy would be free enough from life's responsibilities and constant pressures. Widening your world, indeed, is not about becoming a full-time researcher. It is, however, about committing to do your best. That means seeking out as much information as you can, according to your own circumstances and temperament. It means, especially, not disregarding the information you uncover.

Suppose that you're at the mall and find a truly sumptuous shirt. It's the first one you've really wanted in a long while, and perfect for a party this coming weekend. But then your eyes glance at the label, and you recall that the manufacturer has recently been cited for employing child laborers. Do you buy it anyway and put those children out of your mind? Do you decide, in order to feel okay about buying it, to make a contribution to a child welfare group? Do you sigh longingly and put it back on the rack? Do you tell the manager why you're not buying it and hope the information makes it to the right people? Or, do you race from the store pulling your hair out because all this is too much to bear?

While there's no one right choice to make, there are two keys to arriving at the right choice for *you*. The first key is to remain open and patient, paying specific attention to the common forms of resistance that may arise. Perhaps you'll go numb and deny the social implications of your purchase, as in *I want that shirt and I don't are about anything else.* Perhaps you'll feel bitterness and futility, as in *What difference does it make? Everything you buy is tainted in one way or another.* Perhaps you'll feel fear, as in *I'll never be able to get nice clothes again!* And perhaps you'll feel overwhelm, as in *I can't be the one to solve this problem. I hardly know anything about it.*

The second key in making a choice is to ask your heart. By moving through the kinds of resistance listed above, you'll be able to perceive your heart's true answer. An unwillingness to ask your heart, by contrast, is a sign that you're out of your integrity. To be out of your integrity means that you already sense the answer, but at least temporarily refuse to abide by it.

When you choose to abide by your heart, some of your selves may not like the decision. If you decide to pass up the shirt, for example, you may experience some sadness, regret, or even anger. In the process, you'd come to see that compassionate action doesn't require the actual *feeling* of compassion. Like love, compassion is far more than an emotion. It's an orientation, a lifelong practice. The epitome of the practice is choosing to do no harm especially when you don't feel like it.

Are there any aspects of your life, large or small, that don't fully resonate with your heart? What would bring that resonance about? Can you begin to make it happen, even just a little at a time? If not, can you find and release whatever resistance is in the way? These questions are subtle, complex, and can't be answered all at once. As you change, your answers are likely to change also. That's why it's important not just to ask the questions now, but often.

TAKING LIFE

Are you able to love

what you kill?

*I*n keeping with their vow to do as little harm as possible, people often oppose capital punishment, shun violence, stop eating meat, and object to hunting. These positions, however, aren't mandated by the Seventh Invitation. What the Invitation does mandate is a daring inquiry into the cycle of life and death.

In order to live, you must kill. There's no way around it. If you become a vegetarian, your every meal will require the slaughter of innocent plants. You may think of plants as less conscious than animals, and therefore a better dietary choice, but such reasoning doesn't mitigate the murder. The members of one spiritual sect go so far as to wear masks over their mouths to keep from accidentally ingesting airborne insects. All the while, though, with each scratch of the leg or rub of the forehead, they unwittingly destroy thousands of microscopic creatures.

Killing is ubiquitous, whether purposeful or not. Driving your car, riding your bike, or just walking takes countless lives. Sometimes killing even coexists with peaceful, restorative activities. In tending your garden on a beautiful summer day, you execute weed after helpless weed with every twist and pull.

The reason for accentuating all this carnage is that loving people often get very squeamish about it. This squeamishness can create great resistance to those who kill with less care. It can also lead to the oversimplification of very complex issues.

Take hunting, for example. To target one of God's creatures and then blast it with a bullet can, to some, seem inexcusable. But how many who abhor hunting are more than willing to order tastily cooked animals in restaurants? What about the wretched existence of such factory-farmed animals? What about, for those who select a meatless alternative, the habitat decline caused by pesticides? Is a hunter who honors his prey and partakes of all its gifts more or less humane?

The issue of animal experimentation gives rise to even greater complications. It's almost unbearable to watch videos of animals sickened and then sacrificed to science. Yet how much more unbearable would it be to watch fellow human beings die painful and needless deaths that such experiments could easily prevent? It's one thing to be against animal experimentation in principle, and another when the lives of loved ones are at stake.

Just as love and judgment don't mix, neither do love and self-righteousness. No one's hands are entirely clean. No opinion is entirely right. Whenever killing is involved, even people who embrace all seven Invitations with equal passion may still find themselves on opposing sides. Is this confusing? Maddening? It is, to some degree, for almost everyone seeking to grow in compassion. What, then, does the wisdom of love have to offer?

Faced with the reality that living life means taking life, love as always counsels acceptance. Opening to the killer you are allows you to kill with awareness, to find your own unique distinction between necessary and avoidable death.

From the perspective of an open heart, all life is holy. Any life you take is worthy of honor and blessing. That applies to the weed you pull, the fly you swat, and the mouse you trap. If you can't love what you kill, it means that for some reason you're shut down. There's important resistance to recognize and release.

Any life taken on your behalf is also worthy of honor and blessing. That includes the food on your plate, the shirt on your back, and the wood on your fire. How and when you bestow such appreciation is a deeply personal matter. But whenever you do it's a sacred service. You help keep the world in balance, and at the same time find your place within it.

GUIDELINES FOR GIVING

Real help is resistance free.

W*hat shall I do to serve the world?* Once you accept the Seventh Invitation, seeking to spread love and compassion wherever it's required, this is the obvious question. But there's another, even more important question: *How shall I go about it?* Rather than strategies and methods, this inquiry is about your frame of reference and self-understanding.

Suppose a dear friend of yours has plunged into a period of despair. It hurts to see him this way, and naturally you'd like to help. But why, exactly? Is it so he'll stop hurting, or so that you can? To recognize both possibilities is the first step of true compassion. The second step, before reaching out, is to look for resistance in your own response.

Earlier we discussed many forms of resistance to global suffering, but in a situation so close to home your response may be much simpler. You may just be resisting the feeling of hurt that comes from seeing your friend in pain. This may cause you to act out, to try goading your friend into a happier state of mind. If so, what might seem like caring on the surface could in fact add insult to injury.

Instead of acting out, you could decide to face your resistance. You could locate and feel all the hurt that your friend's despair has stirred. Choosing to do so would lay the groundwork for true communion. It may lead you to forgo offering advice and just listen. You may learn that his current depression is less a crisis and more part of a natural cycle. You may find that just the act of asking questions, rather than imposing your own agenda, is what's necessary to get him unstuck. Or, when all is said and done, he may indeed respond to genuine good cheer.

Let's imagine now that your friend's woes are self-created. Perhaps he cheated on his wife and shattered his marriage. Your response to his despair, in this case, might have a lot to do with how you view infidelity. If you disapprove of it, there might be a hostile edge to your tone. Or perhaps, unconsciously, the guidance you offer would be less about real help and more about making your friend feel bad.

Any such judgment would result from resistance, and would clearly be a disservice to your friend. What's less loving, after all, than blame in the guise of support? What's more loving, on the other hand, than to reveal yourself with complete candor? Imagine being able to communicate the following: "I want to be the best friend I can to you, but I recognize how much this situation triggers me. I'm working on that. Meanwhile, if my words ever feel slanted, or at all reactive, please let me know right away." You might decide, of course, that your friend is currently too fragile to hear such an admission. But even if that's the case, you can still keep it uppermost in your mind.

From the above examples come the two most important guidelines in offering any type of assistance. First, strive to find every possible resistance within your view of an external issue. This creates a relationship of equality rather than superiority, and is precisely what makes working on yourself and the world one and the same. Second, before offering help of any kind, picture yourself as the recipient of that help. Rather than role playing yourself into the recipient's shoes, imagine that the situation is truly reversed and that this help is being offered to you. Give this exercise enough time for all your selves to weigh in, from the most familiar to the most overlooked, from the most celebrated to the most shadowed. If anything about the offer would seem counterproductive to even just one of your selves, or would needlessly incite such a self to resist, then hold off and give the situation more thought.

Reflect upon the last time you gave someone aid or advice. Did it meet these guidelines? If not, step back into the scene and examine your response. If you fell short regarding the first guideline, see if you can recognize the resistance that clouded your perception. If you fell short of the second guideline, take a moment and try to grasp how it would've felt for you, all of you, to be in the other person's shoes at that time. Once your exploration is complete, envision yourself offering the same aid or advice again. Is it different in content, tone, or both? Does it seem likely to be more effective?

Once you've followed these guidelines in your personal life, it's then possible to apply them to social concerns. To demonstrate, let's look at the subject of welfare reform. Those who need welfare are dependent upon you as a taxpayer for their survival. How you respond to their need is determined in large part by how you relate to your own needs. Do you find it difficult to ask for help? Does depending on others feel wrong, or shameful? If so, and if you resist these feelings, it may cause you to act out by disparaging welfare recipients. You may support a harsh reduction of benefits. Your position on welfare may also be influenced by the way you view wealth and privilege. Do you feel guilty about your own prosperity? If so, resisting that guilt may cause you to romanticize the poor, and you may support a large benefit increase.

Working through your possible resistance to dependency or privilege would help you play a clear and compassionate role in the movement for welfare reform. To do so would entail opening to whatever emotions are involved, and searching for any one-sided self-judgments or limiting core beliefs that may be blocking them. If those emotions need a nudge to get moving, you could embody them in the same way that you played out your hostility on pages 205 to 206. You could also scan your past for any challenging events that may have narrowed your views on this topic, then expand those memories to free you up. And finally, you could give a complete airing to any selves that have a particularly strong stake in this issue. If necessary, you could embody these selves with complete abandon, just as you've learned to play the roles of emotions and other people.

At this point you'd have the first guideline totally covered and could move on to the second. This means applying it to any prospective policy. Even the best policy, if it doesn't create an environment for success, is almost certain to fail. If your goal was not just to reduce the welfare rolls but also to provide meaningful opportunities for welfare recipients, you'd need to know whether the people affected by this policy would feel dignified, encouraged, and hopeful, or worthless, rebuked, and defeated. Stepping into their shoes, and imagining the policy's impact on all your own selves, would provide valuable understanding in this regard.

The next time you encounter an initiative about any social issue—such as AIDS, the war on drugs, homelessness, assisted suicide—don't settle for your instinctive response. And don't turn to the usual sources of debate either. Instead, evaluate the idea with the two guidelines for giving and see if it holds up. If it does, and you're for it, this discovery may spur you to lend a hand. If it doesn't, see if you can determine precisely why not. Sometimes it's just a matter of implementation and only pertains to the second guideline. But often the first guideline is where the problem lies.

A proposed law or program may reflect the resistance of a whole community, state, or even country. The lack of one may do the same. Take the case of AIDS, for example. Before a significant national response was even discussed, thousands of Americans had died of the disease. Because of a deep national resistance to homosexuality, the epidemic spread far more quickly than necessary to all sectors of the population. It's worth restating the difference here between resistance and opposition. Even when opposing homosexuality as a way of life, one could still accept its existence and address the related issues with clarity.

Collective resistance influences how a society treats less powerful groups of all kinds. In addition it influences how the earth is cared for, how enemies are defined, and even how wars are waged. Recognizing collective resistance allows you to draw attention to it, to join forces with those seeking to create a more aware and loving society. It also allows you to find and release any similar resistance within. To some degree it's bound to be there. For just as your view of the world is a reflection of you, so, too, are you a reflection of the world.

THE GOOD FIGHT

Change rarely comes without struggle.

What is the loving response to racism or sexism? What does love ask of us when people are denied sustenance, tortured, or ravaged by ethnic cleansing? Conflict, as we discussed in Two to Tango (page 196), is as important to relationships as it is unpleasant. Conflict is equally important in the pursuit of an equitable world. Frequently, as counterintuitive as this can seem to openhearted people, it's necessary to stand up and fight.

This often means opposing what's done in your name and with your tax dollars. Disapproval of a government policy without seeking an alternative is virtually the same as an endorsement. That's why it's so important to vote, for both candidates and initiatives that represent your views. Sometimes, though, voting is not enough. Your conscience calls you to do more.

In following your conscience no conflict may be necessary. No one may stand in your way. The whole process may surge forward as one great "Yes!" Unfortunately, however, the forces of power and money don't often align with love. Therefore, most of your efforts for change are likely to face significant struggle. To put forth your positive vision, you'll first need to shout a resounding "No!"

Civil rights for African Americans meant shouting "No!" to Jim Crow laws. Passing the Clean Water Act meant shouting "No!" to toxic waste. But the "No!" that succeeds in stopping all forms of injustice is neither bitter nor vindictive. Instead it's rousing, empowering, and exactly what love wants.

What brings about your loving "No!"? What issues make you feel positively electric? Look slowly over the list below, one issue at a time, and see if any call out to you. Pay attention to how your body responds. Watch the nature of your thoughts. Which items on the list, no matter your position, energize you to make change happen?

AIDS
Climate change
Corporate responsibility
Deforestation
Discrimination
Domestic violence
Drugs
Education
Energy
Genetic engineering
Guns
Healthcare
Homelessness
Human rights
Hunger
Landmines
Nuclear weapons
Overpopulation
Pollution
Poverty
Prisons
Sweatshops

If none of these issues light you up, search for others that do. Take note, as well, of issues about which you crave more information. The only thing standing between you and your unique contribution to any fight for change may just be a little more knowledge. How much time each month would you be willing to devote to such an investigation? One hour? Two?

Most of us aren't like John Wallach. Our compassionate action doesn't

come in the form of a breakthrough vision like Seeds of Peace. Having discovered the issues that most inflame our hearts, we seek out small projects and
incremental changes. Instead of trying to save all forests, for instance, most
likely we start with one. Usually our first step is to join with others who share
the same conviction. In addition to providing moral support and the obvious
strength in numbers, working with groups allows us to make friends, build
community, and above all have fun. Groups also allow us to share the load, focusing on the types of involvement for which we're best suited.

Significant fights for change involve endless rounds of research and letter
writing. They require legal battles, outreach, fundraising, and countless meet-
ings. There's always a way to take part, no matter our time or skills. Even if
all other efforts fail, and the group decides to commit civil disobedience, not
everyone joins the frontlines. Those unwilling to risk arrest can still sew ban-
ners, ferry supplies, arrange for bail, or manage the media.

None of this is easy. Speaking truth to power takes great courage. Suffering the consequences entails great sacrifice. Harder still, in the heat of the
moment, is facing our adversaries with a loving heart. To accomplish this requires all the Invitations, as well as all the tools they provide. It is particularly
helpful to revisit the exercises in Compassion, on page 229. In the end, however, nothing is more instrumental than rededication to our one overriding
goal—remaining open to the present moment, and to the love that resides
there eternally. In time, without our needing to attach or direct it, that love
becomes all-inclusive.

No matter how challenging this may get, battling for a better world still
gives much more than it takes. When we fight the good fight, our hearts sing.
When we fight along with others, the chorus swells. When multitudes join
together, the harmony becomes living thunder. Ultimately, we come to grasp
that love, though the most powerful force on earth, can't accomplish a thing
without us.

A HEART ON FIRE

Nothing can eclipse love's light.

Sometimes, no matter how important the cause, we just don't want to fight. We want to rejoice in the unity we feel rather than combat the division we see. We want to live a quiet and loving life, do as little harm as possible, and leave the world's monumental struggles to others. Often, especially if our road to love has been long and arduous, all we want to do is stop, rest, and retreat.

Do you feel that way periodically? Do you find yourself letting the morning paper stack up unread, or switching channels to avoid the news? Self-care and rejuvenation are vital parts of a balanced and healthy life, but they can also become numbing habits. Amid the bombardment of contemporary culture we can grow accustomed to tuning out. We can end up addicted to comfort, and in the process choose complacency over love.

This may sound like a demand to be stronger, to do more, but actually it isn't. After you've accepted all Seven Invitations, love is no longer hard work. The rediscovery of your true and loving nature is complete. Your actions begin effortlessly to reflect that. The only thing required from now on, even at the most daunting times, is that you surrender your will to your heart.

Surrender, in this case, means soliciting your heart at every turn. It means, literally, placing the fullness of your attention at the source of love within you, and then letting that love steer your life. When you do so, the right course of action will either radiate directly from love or ring resoundingly with it. This applies to your overall intention—that larger purpose that guides you forward, as discussed in Lucid Living (page 168)—it also applies to life's small and seemingly less significant moments. It particularly applies whenever you feel yourself susceptible to complacency. The very act of surrender is what brings forth the resolve you lack. In its aftermath love leads the way, love does the work, and you become its living vessel.

The idea that love is effortless bears careful explanation, especially after each succeeding Invitation has encouraged you to stretch even more than the one before. There's no doubt that to reach this point you've expended great effort, but it was all about removing obstacles and getting out of the way. As a result, most of your accumulated and habitual forms of resistance have been released. You therefore recognize any newly arising resistance almost immediately, and can move through whatever it's blocking with ease.

Because of your ongoing commitment to this process, you're also more fully able to stop trying, to relax your way into love as we first discussed in A Deep Breath on page 65. This eliminates the majority of interference between you and your heart. You're able to discern and trust your heart's guidance. Your heart, in turn, is able to spur you on and sustain you all at once. In keeping with this mission, it will not ask of you what you can't accomplish. It will not take from you what it won't supply.

Think about a time in your life when someone you loved needed help, and that help seemed impossible to give. Perhaps you were sick or already overburdened, but saying no was just out of the question. Somehow, you held out your hand. Somehow, you both made it through. Even if it seemed like your offering was a triumph of will, in fact it was a triumph of love. Love was what generated the will. And that miracle, fleeting though it was at the time, can now be your way of life.

To experience this firsthand, try the following. Pick up a newspaper and read through every article about a social problem or crisis. Let all your resistance to each issue come and go, let all your feelings come and go, and then solicit your heart's response. Sometimes it may just offer a brief prayer, or simple good wishes for those involved. Other times it may prompt you to share the information with friends. If it's a far-reaching issue, such as global warming, your heart may call for small personal responses like turning down your thermostat or buying a more fuel-efficient car. And in some cases your heart may flare, signaling the need for a more direct and long-term contribution.

If such a contribution exceeds your available energy, ask your heart for more. Don't push. Wait for the energy to come. Inevitably, it will. And when the project drags on and your energy begins to wane, ask for more still. When the need to ask seems too frequent, revisit your heart's original calling. It may have changed. It may be time to place your energy elsewhere.

While writing this book, as I described in the Introduction, it was necessary for me to listen to my heart. Now, as the book comes to a close, it's time to add to that description. Often the writing process was very difficult. I felt humbled by the responsibility. There were days, even weeks, when the words just wouldn't come, or when they felt unworthy of my heart's intent. As someone used to gritting it out, to solving problems through sheer persistence, I would respond to these dry spells by trying harder. It never succeeded, and in fact usually made things worse. But along the way, heeding the Invitations even as I composed them, I learned to stop trying. I learned to place all my attention on my heart, to surrender to it without pressure or demand. When I did, the right words would consistently flow. The larger a vessel I made myself for love, the more love came surging through.

This discovery, of course, is in no way unique to me. It's been the underlying theme on every page. Rather than something we need to create, love is infinite and always present. Rather than something for us to give or receive, love offers itself through a fiery heart.

When your heart is on fire, it can burn through every challenge. No amount of compassion, service, or struggle is beyond its flame. Whenever you begin to doubt this, to wander away from the light, simply remember:

Feel Everything
Question Everything
Resist Nothing
Live Like You're Dying

Live Like You're Dreaming
Love Like You're Dancing
Widen Your World

By accepting each of love's Invitations, you offer your own invitation to love.

ACCEPTING THE

SEVENTH INVITATION

To the best of my current and evolving ability, I resolve to:

- Acknowledge global interdependence
- Break through my blocks to compassion
- Inflict the least harm possible
- Honor the lives I take
- Abide by the guidelines for giving
- Become a force for necessary change
- Surrender my will to my heart

BENEDICTION

May your presence always deepen

May your exploration never cease

May not a speck of God's creation elude your heart's embrace

May you live as you die—awake, ablaze

May you live as you dream—garbed in miracles

May you explode with loving light, in the mirror of your beloveds

And may the sparks rain down forever toward an undivided world

GRATITUDE

*T*he existence of this book is a testament to its own subject matter. It would not have been possible without the love and support of countless individuals. While some of them are my family members and close friends, others I've only met with briefly during talks, workshops, and one-on-one sessions. Every openhearted connection over the past two years, no matter how seemingly fleeting, has touched me indelibly and helped birth these Invitations. To all of you who welcomed me in this way, my gratitude is unceasing.

I offer an additional bow of appreciation to those who shepherded the manuscript from inception to completion. First among them is Amy Elizabeth Fox, who heard the music before there were even instruments, and made sure everyone else did, too. Next there was Eileen Cope of Lowenstein Associates, devoted agent and magical opener of doors. Then there was Marta-Maria Marraccini, who listened and listened, read and read, and gave me months of exquisite support when I could give little in return.

Along with those above, my committee of wise and gracious readers included Astara Briski, Lynda Harvey, Terry Patten, Kate Taylor, and Jane Waxman. Thankfully, they kept sending me back to the drawing board whenever my efforts fell short. Josh Baran, as always, was my unwavering champion throughout. Joel Heller, in particular, held the torch for simplicity and clarity. And my editor at Broadway, Ann Campbell, was unerring in her diligence and vision. I now know firsthand what a "writer's editor" truly is.

STAYING CONNECTED

*A*ny and all communication from readers of this book is encouraged and appreciated. To share your questions, comments, stories, and reflections about setting your own heart on fire, please visit the companion website at:

www.heartonfire.org

This website also provides regularly updated information about *Setting Your Heart on Fire* workshops, retreats, and counseling sessions nationwide. To send correspondence or receive information via the postal service, please write to:

Raphael Cushnir
The Heartfire Foundation
Box 427
Tomales, CA 94971